HALLOWEEN

DOT MARKER ACTIVITY BOOK

FOR KIDS AGES 2+

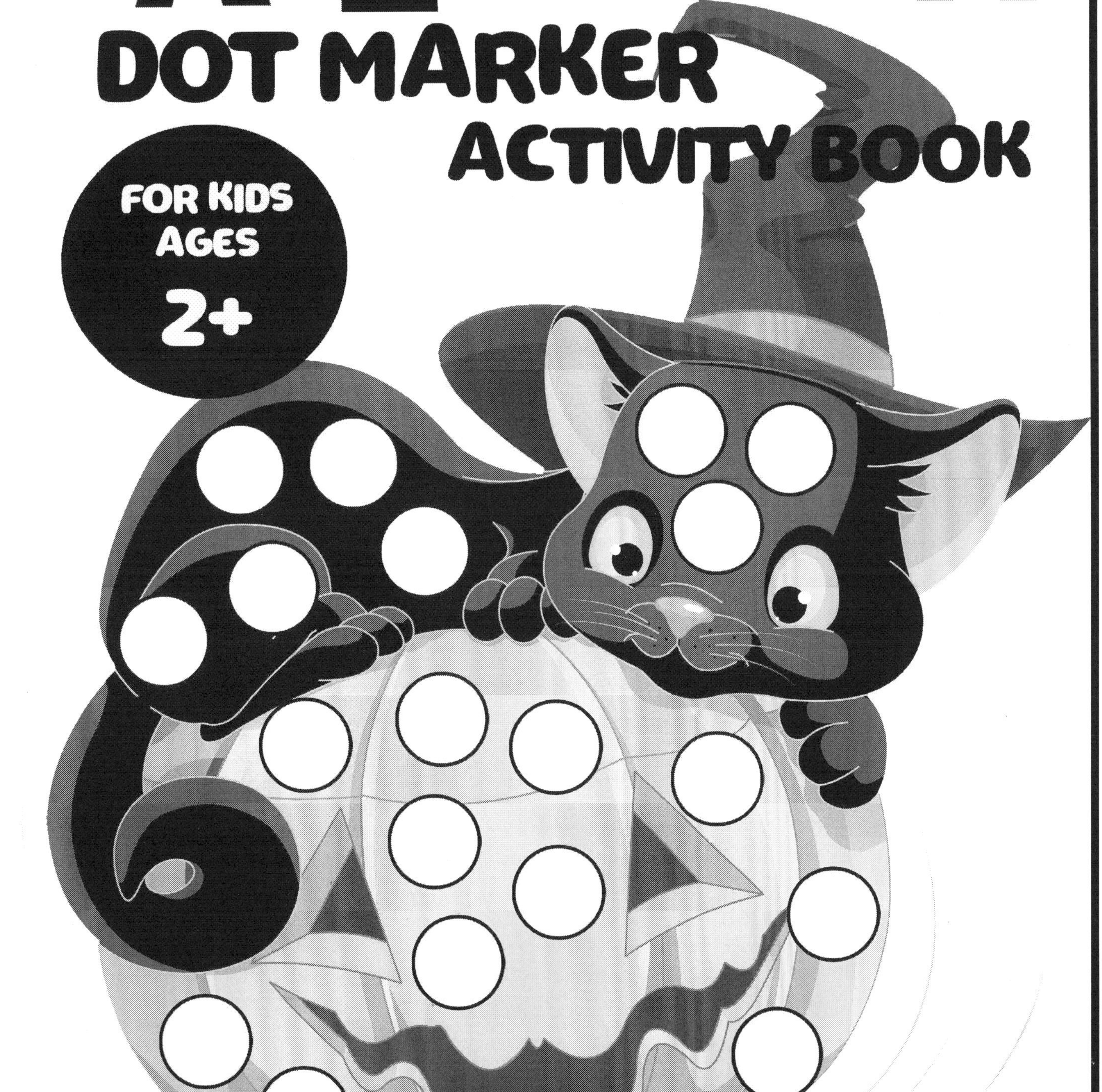

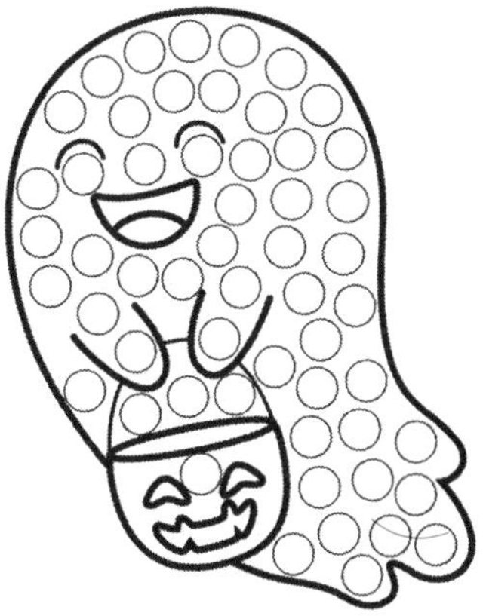

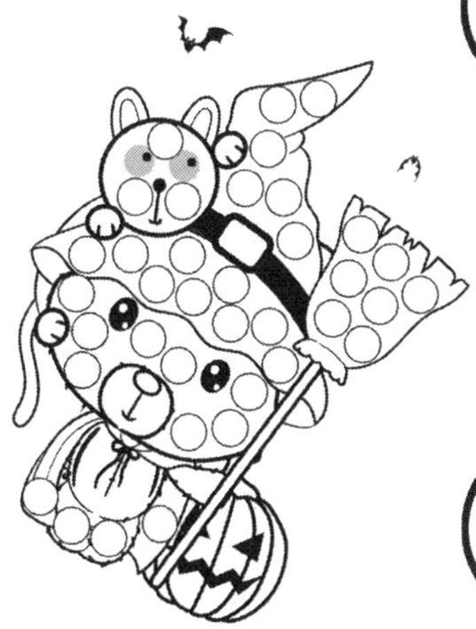

This Book Belongs To:

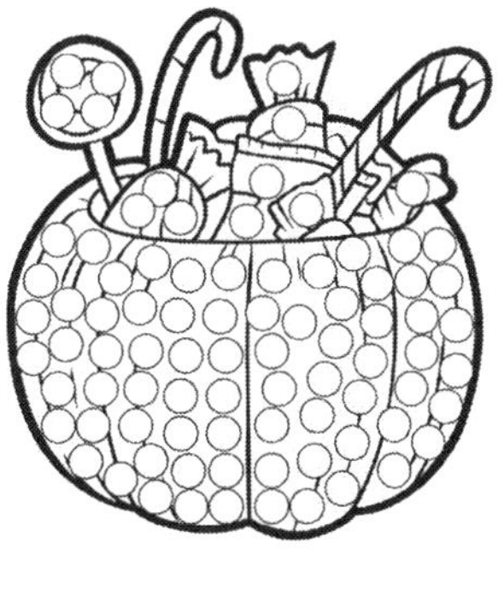

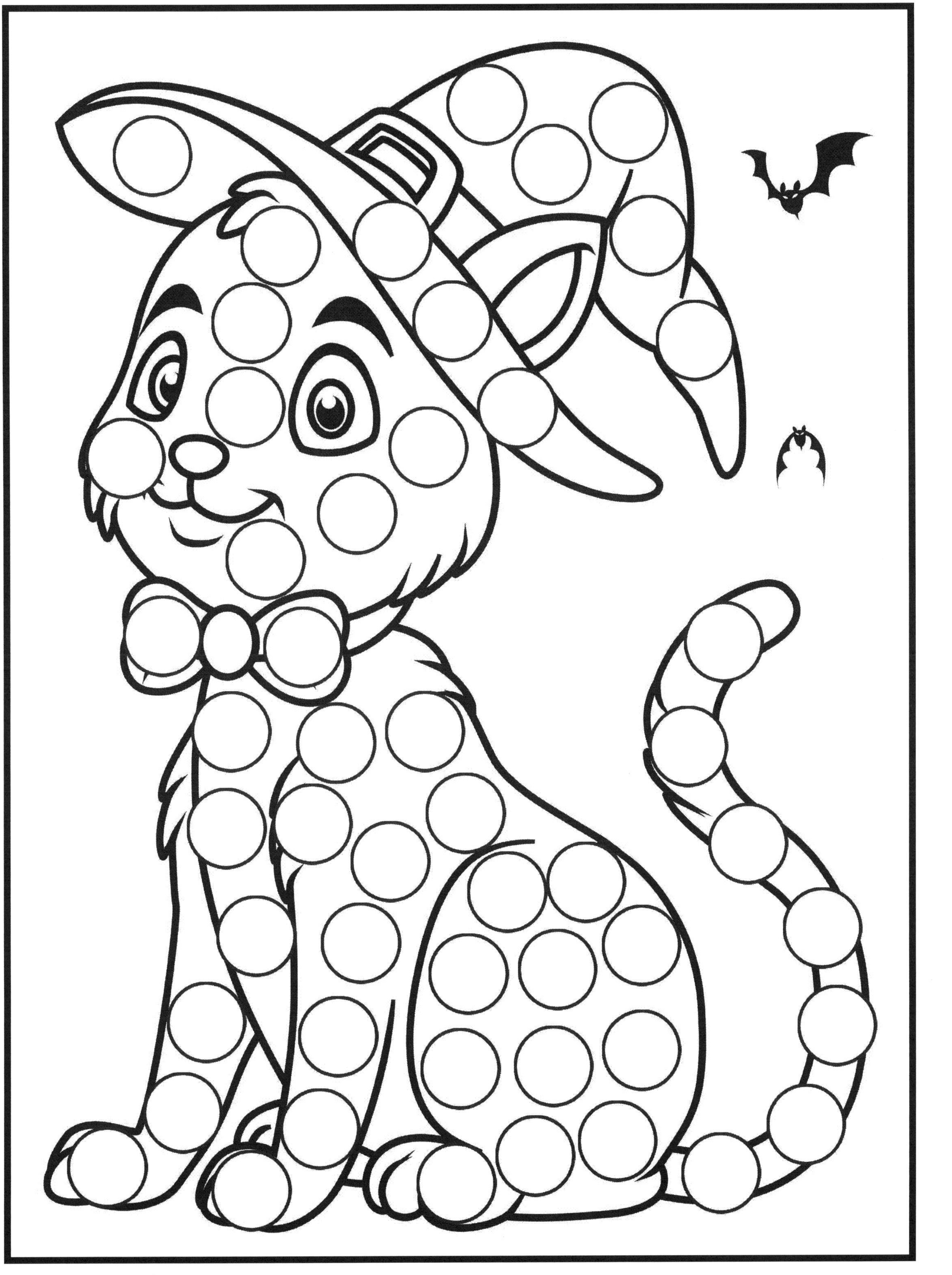

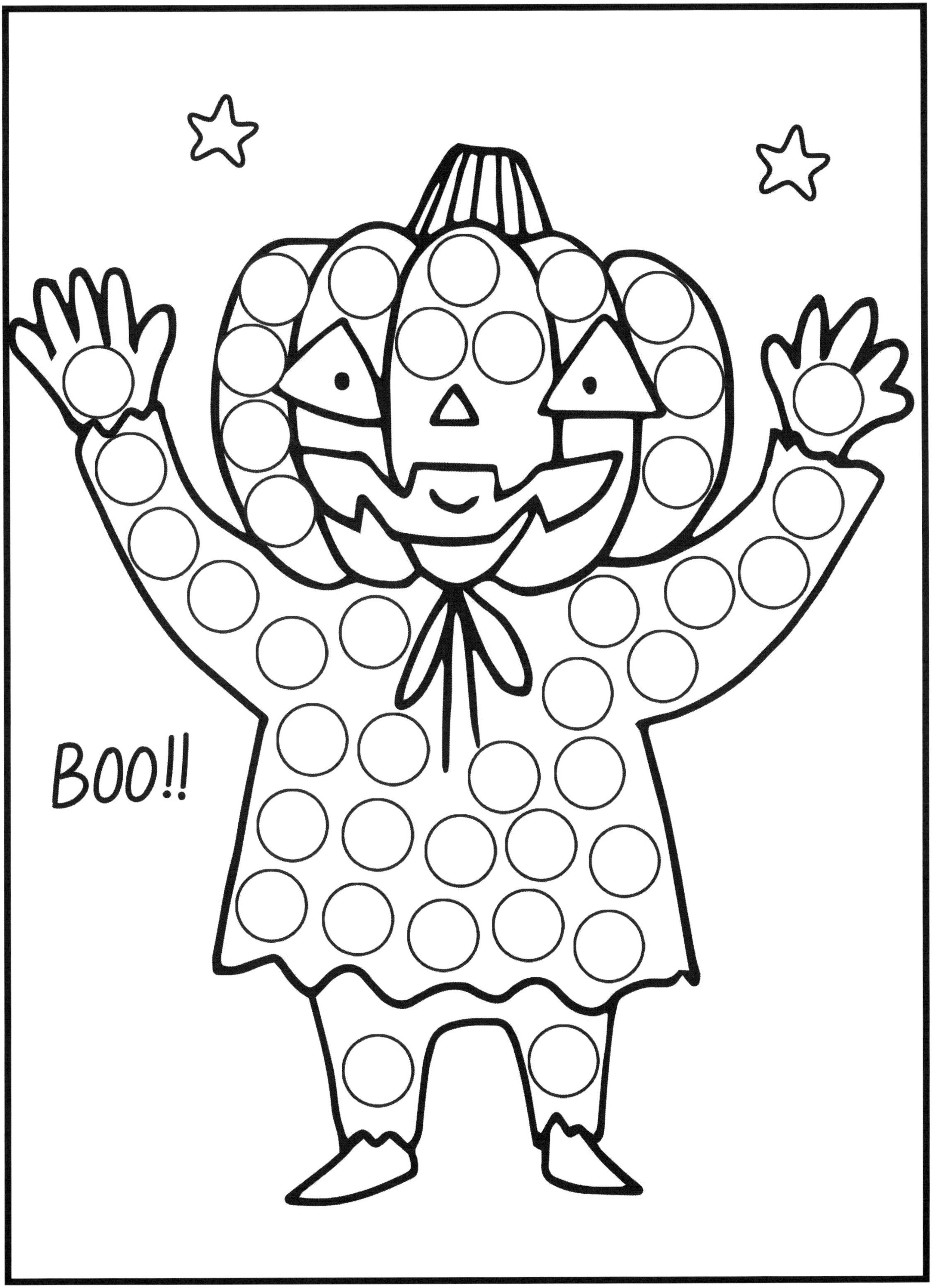
BOO!!

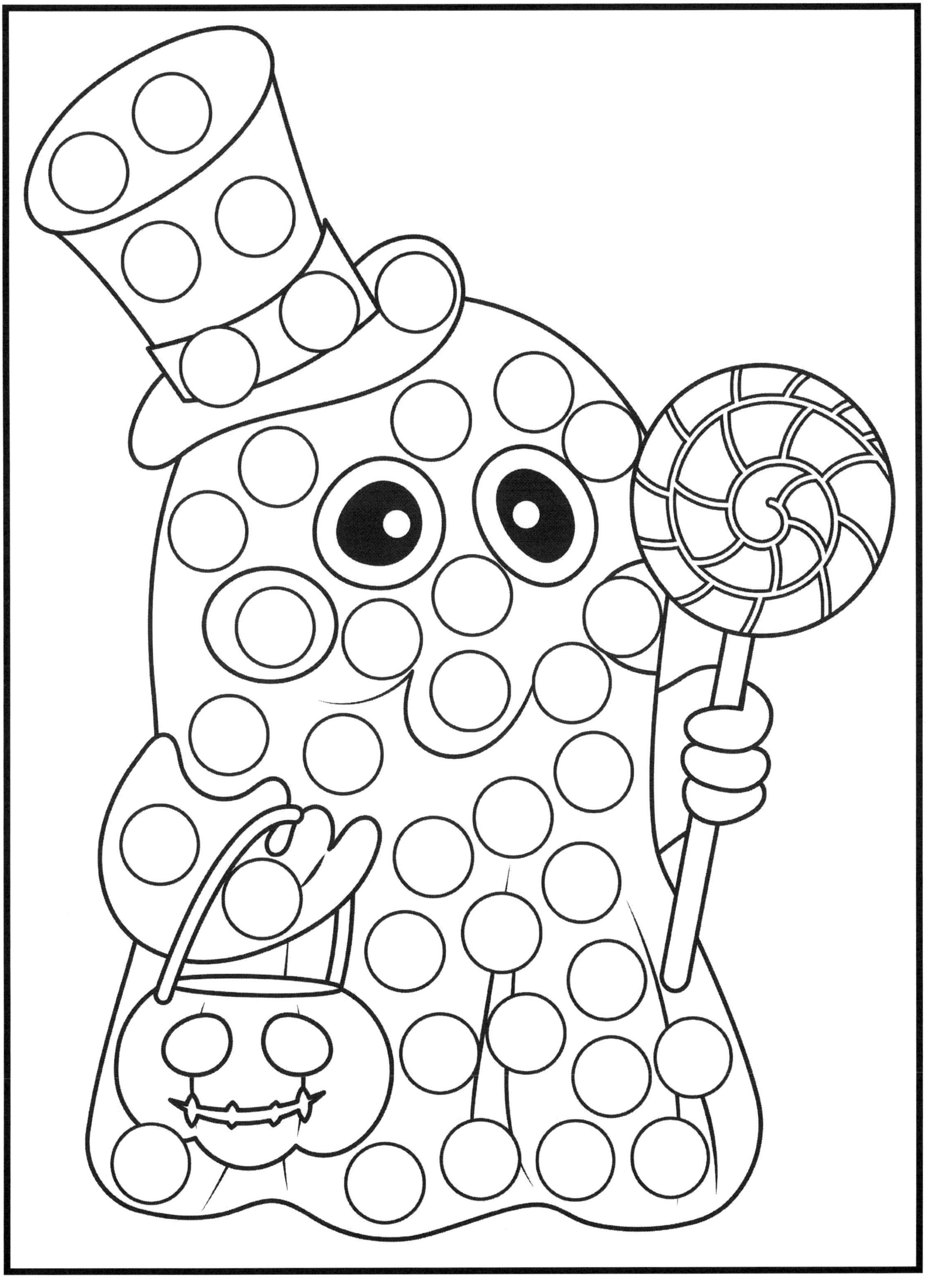

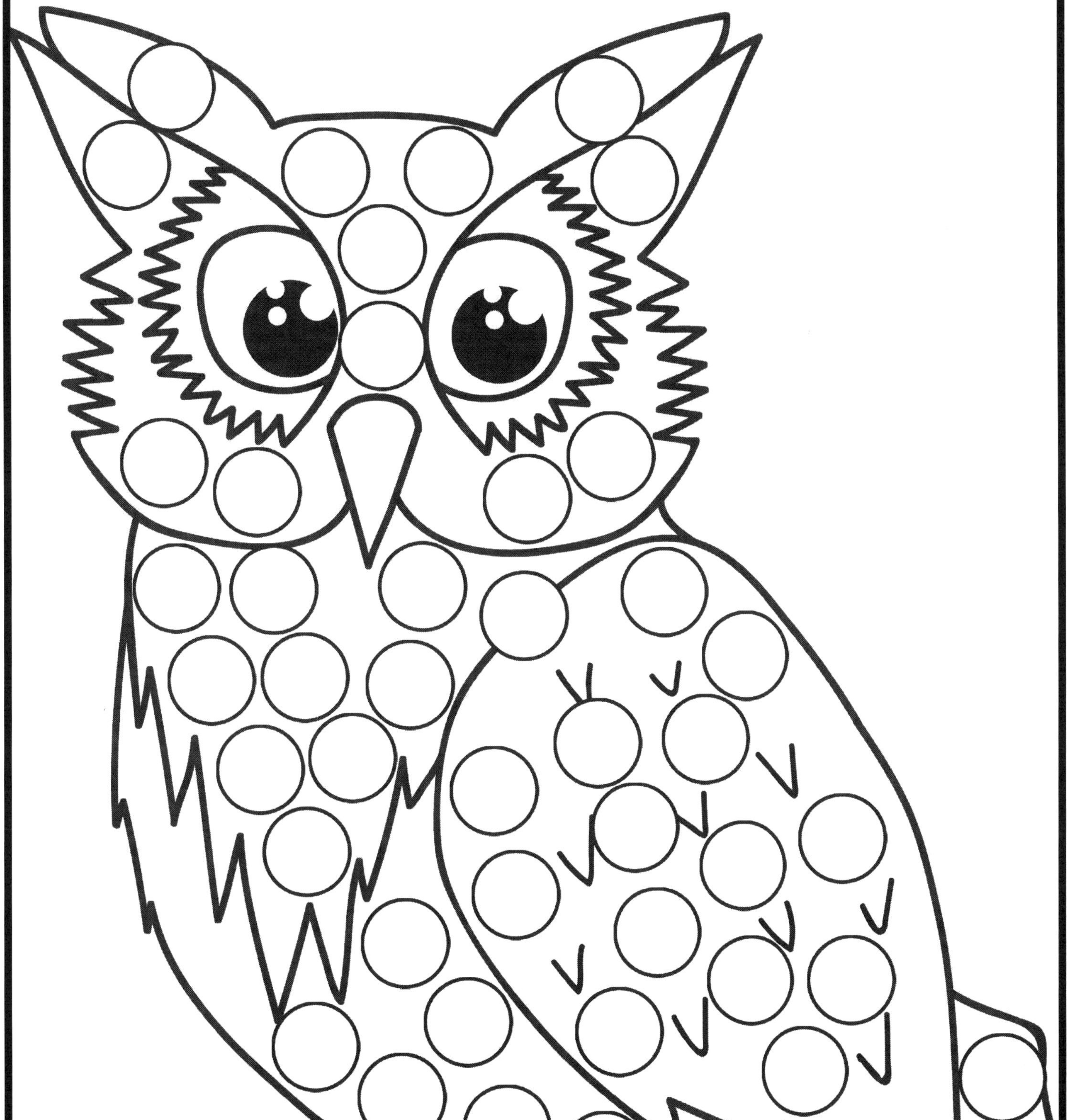

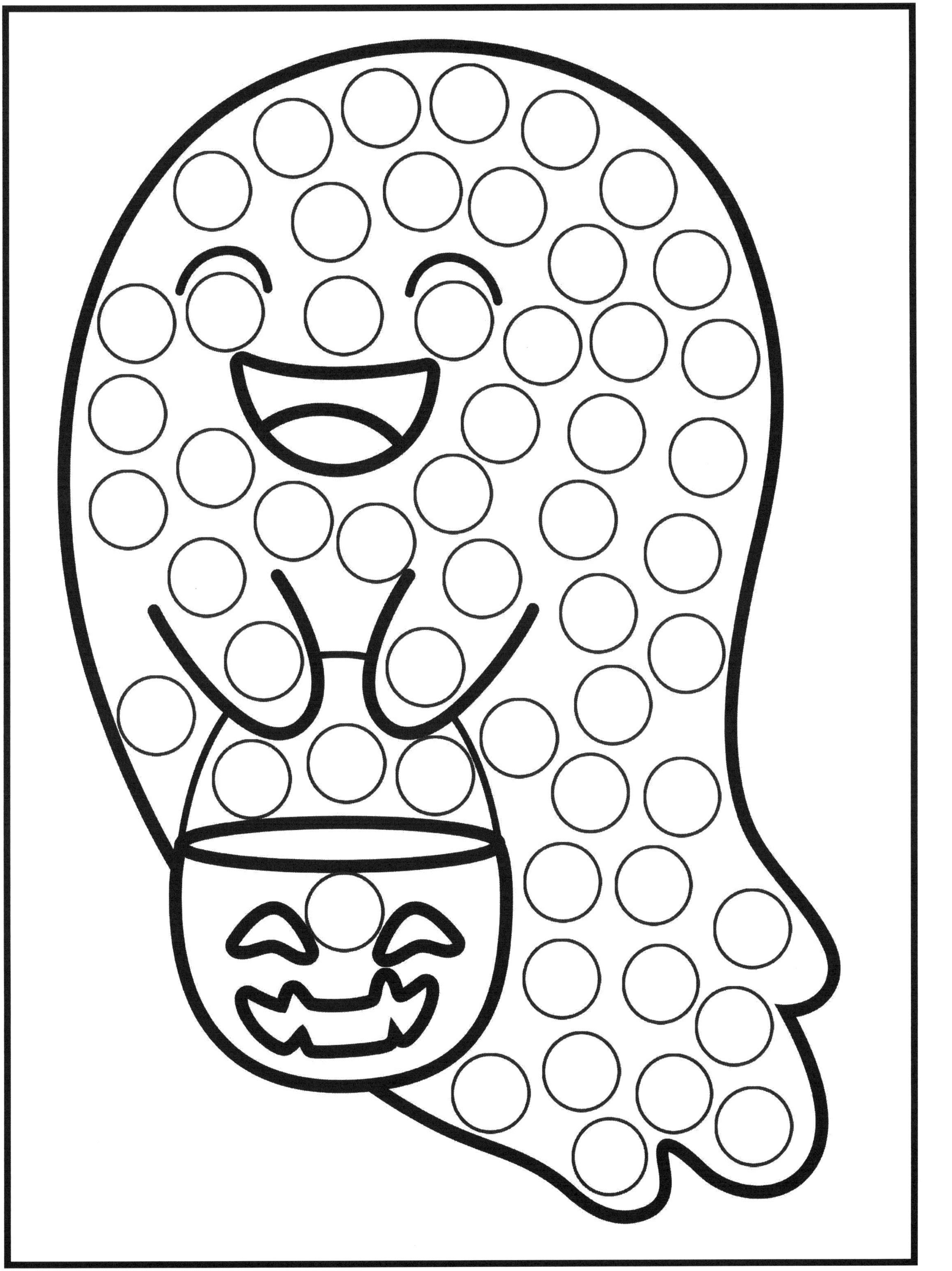

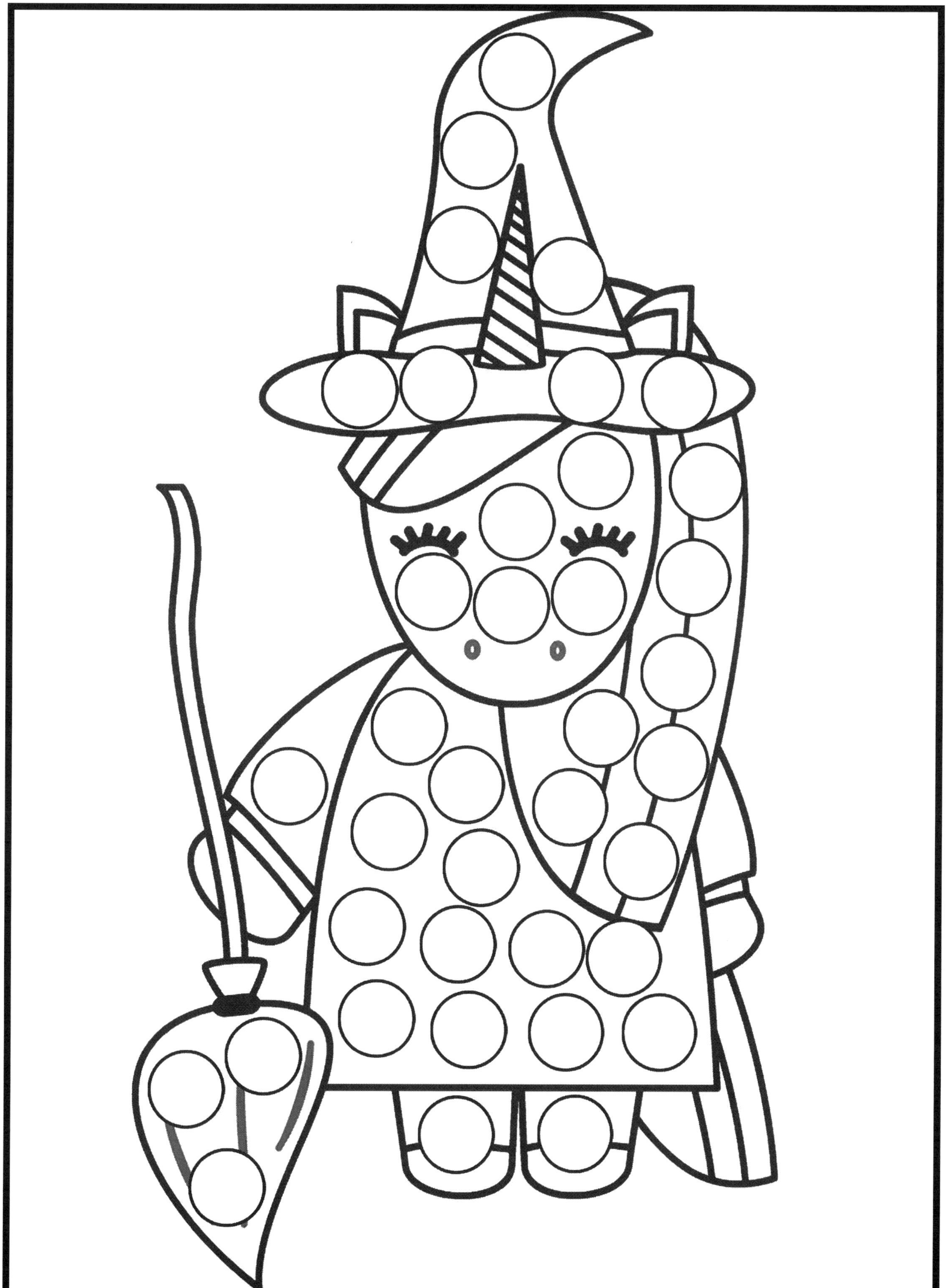

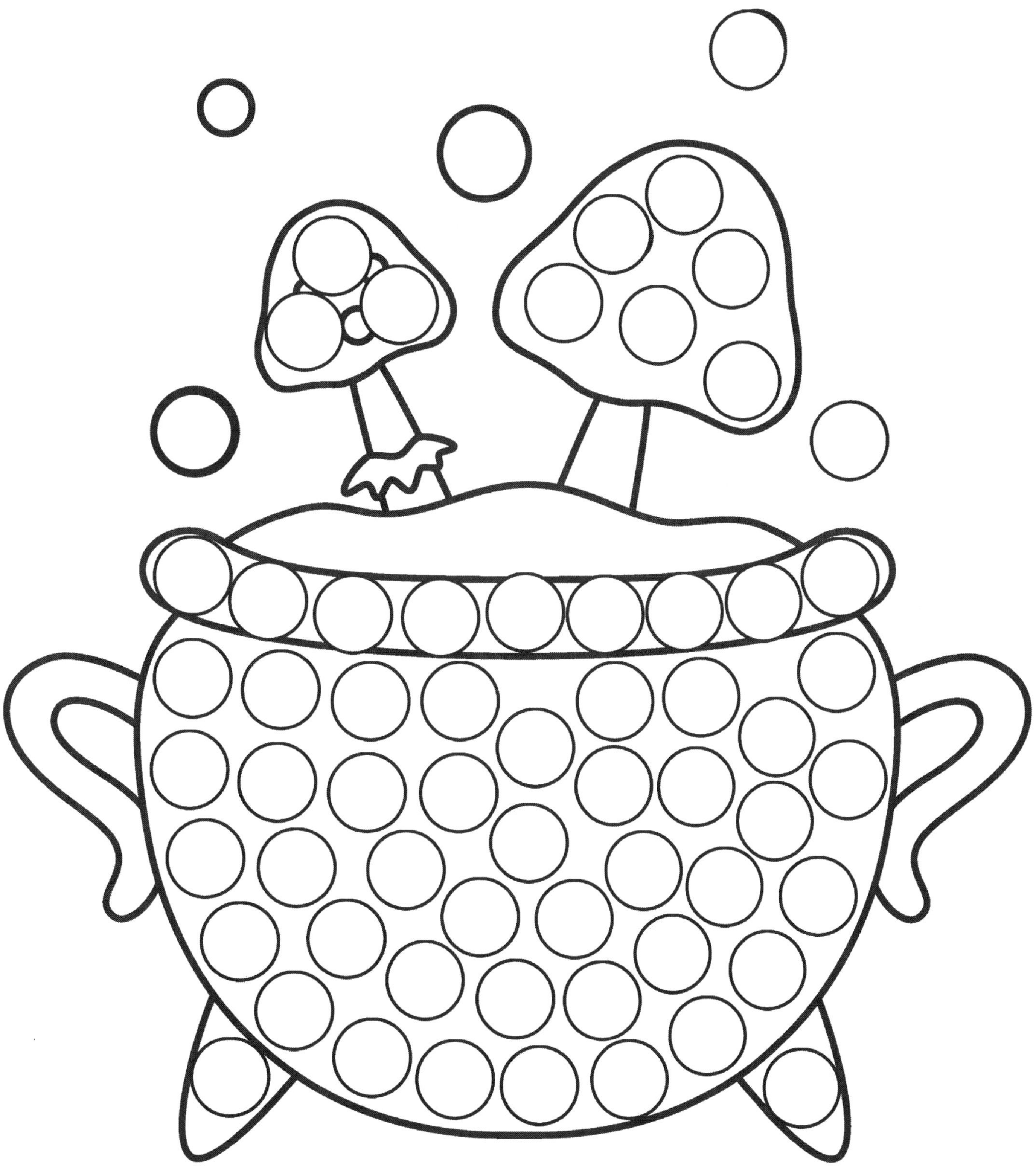

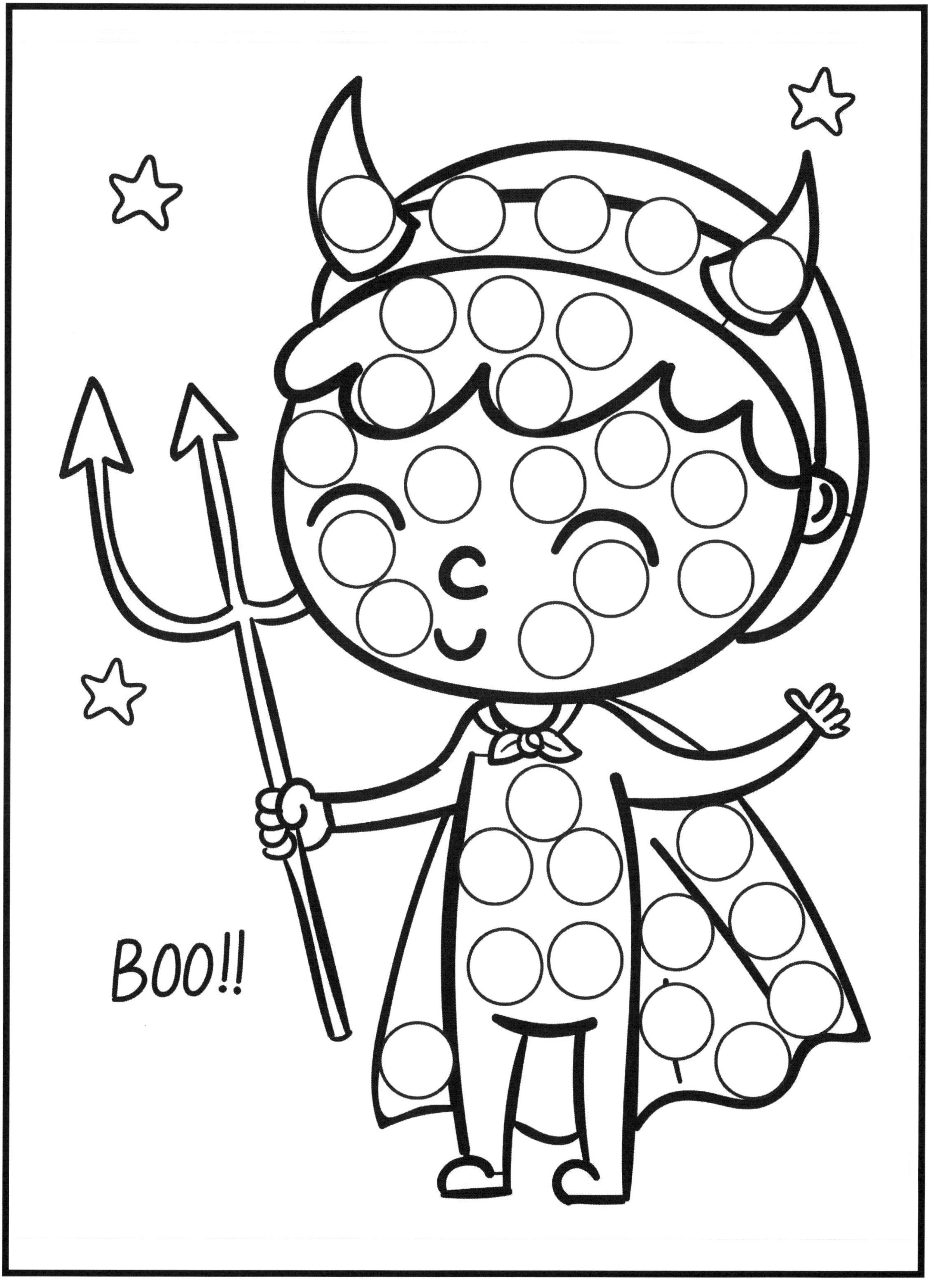
BOO!!

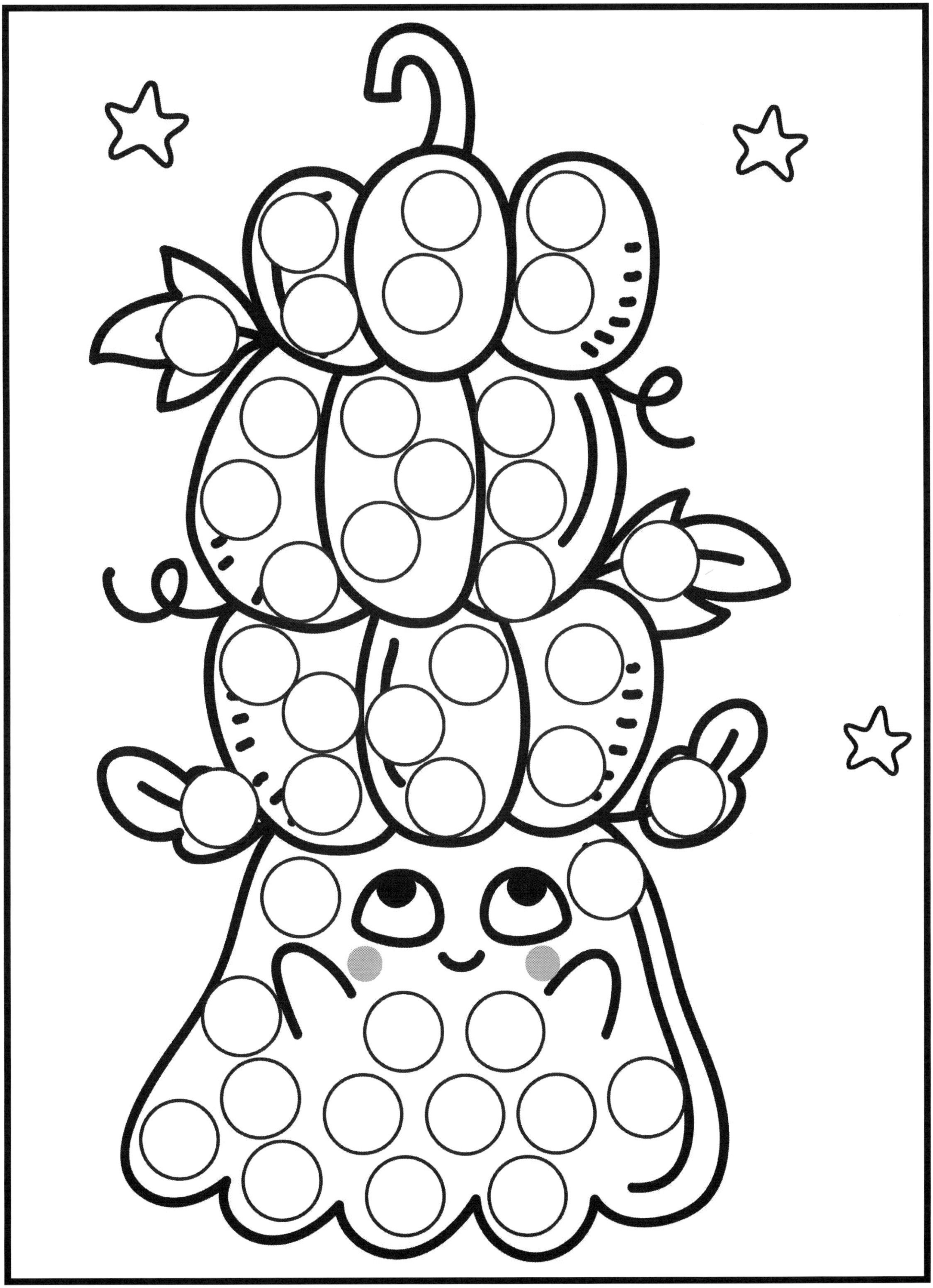

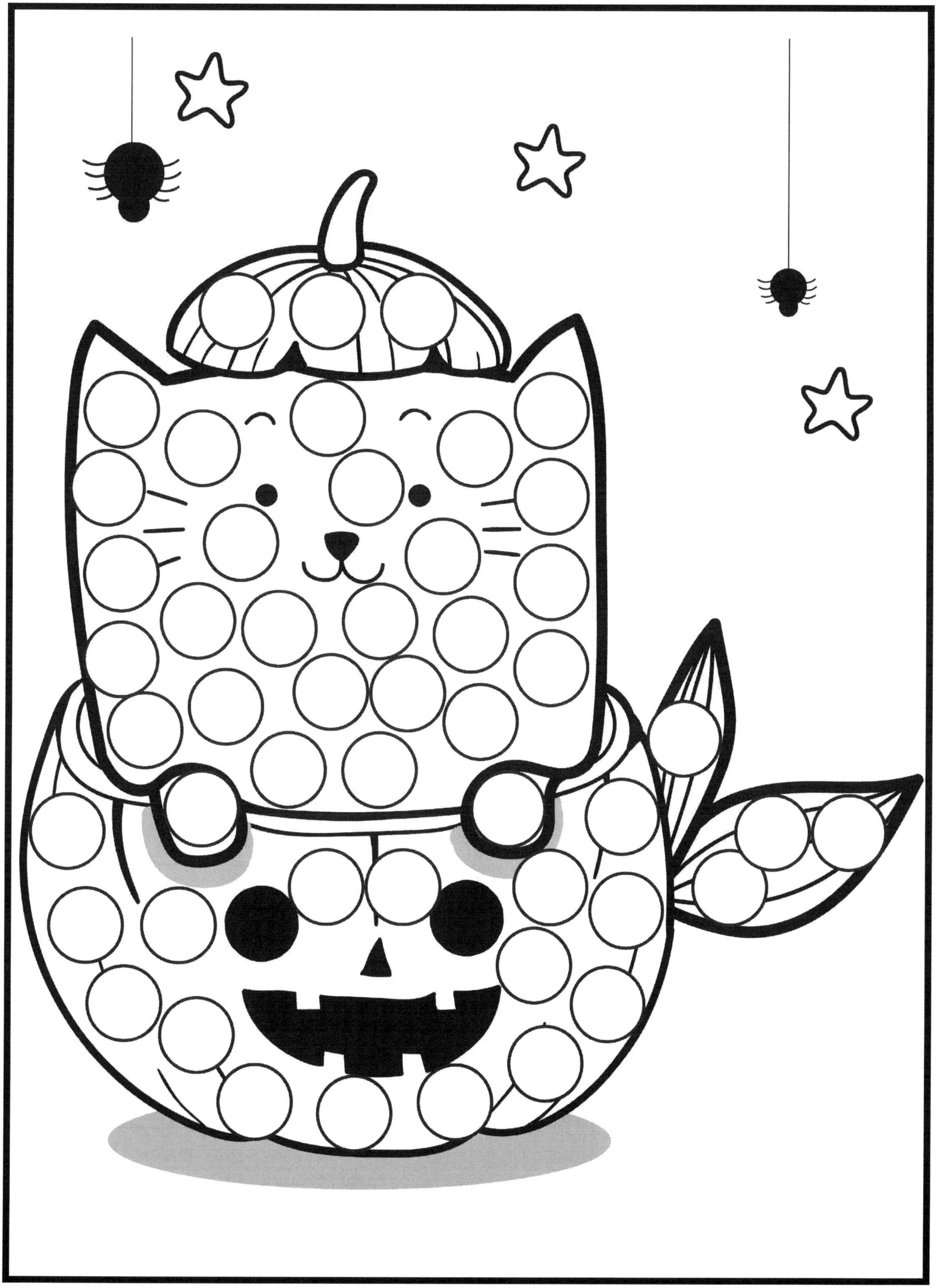

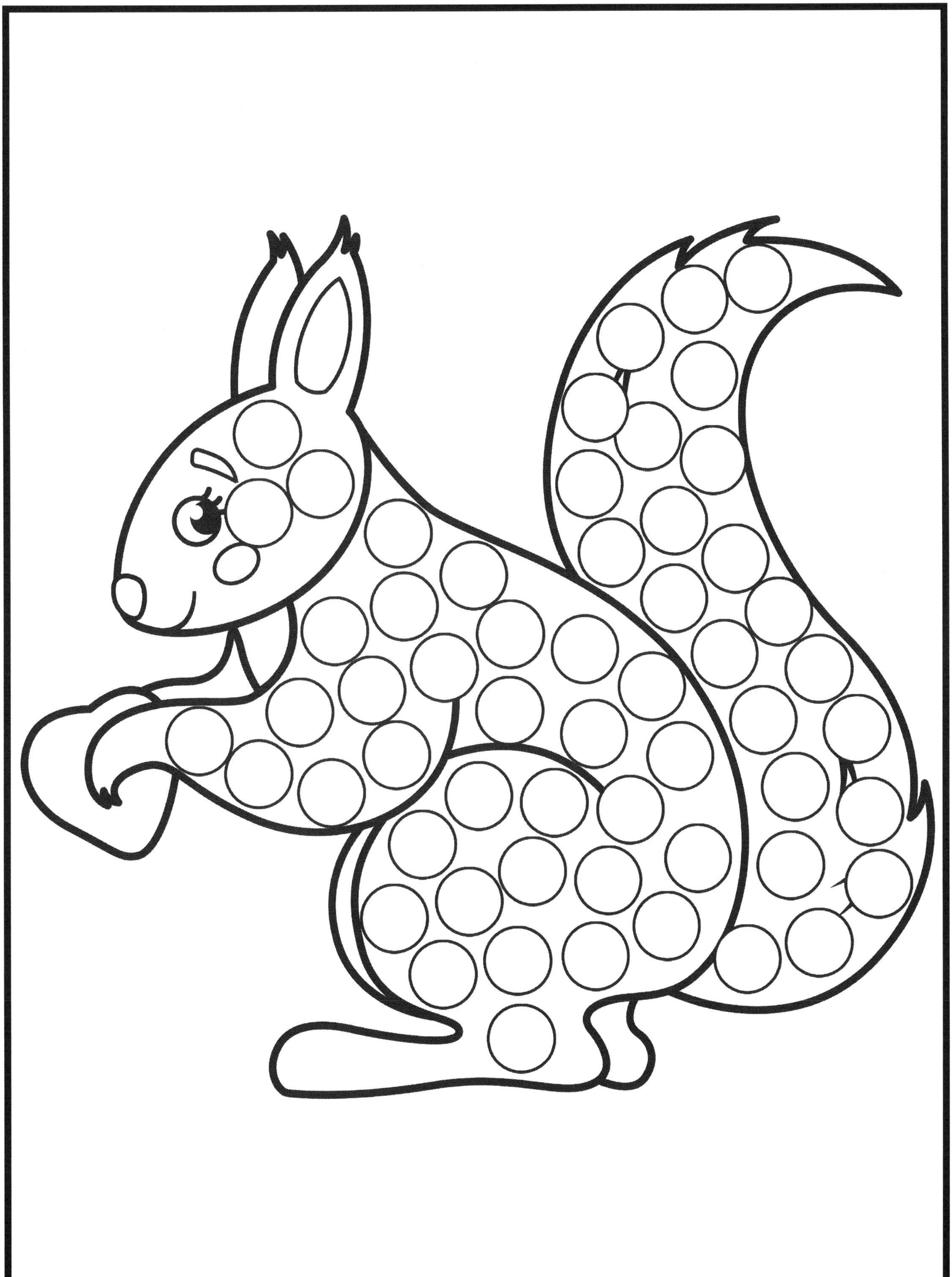

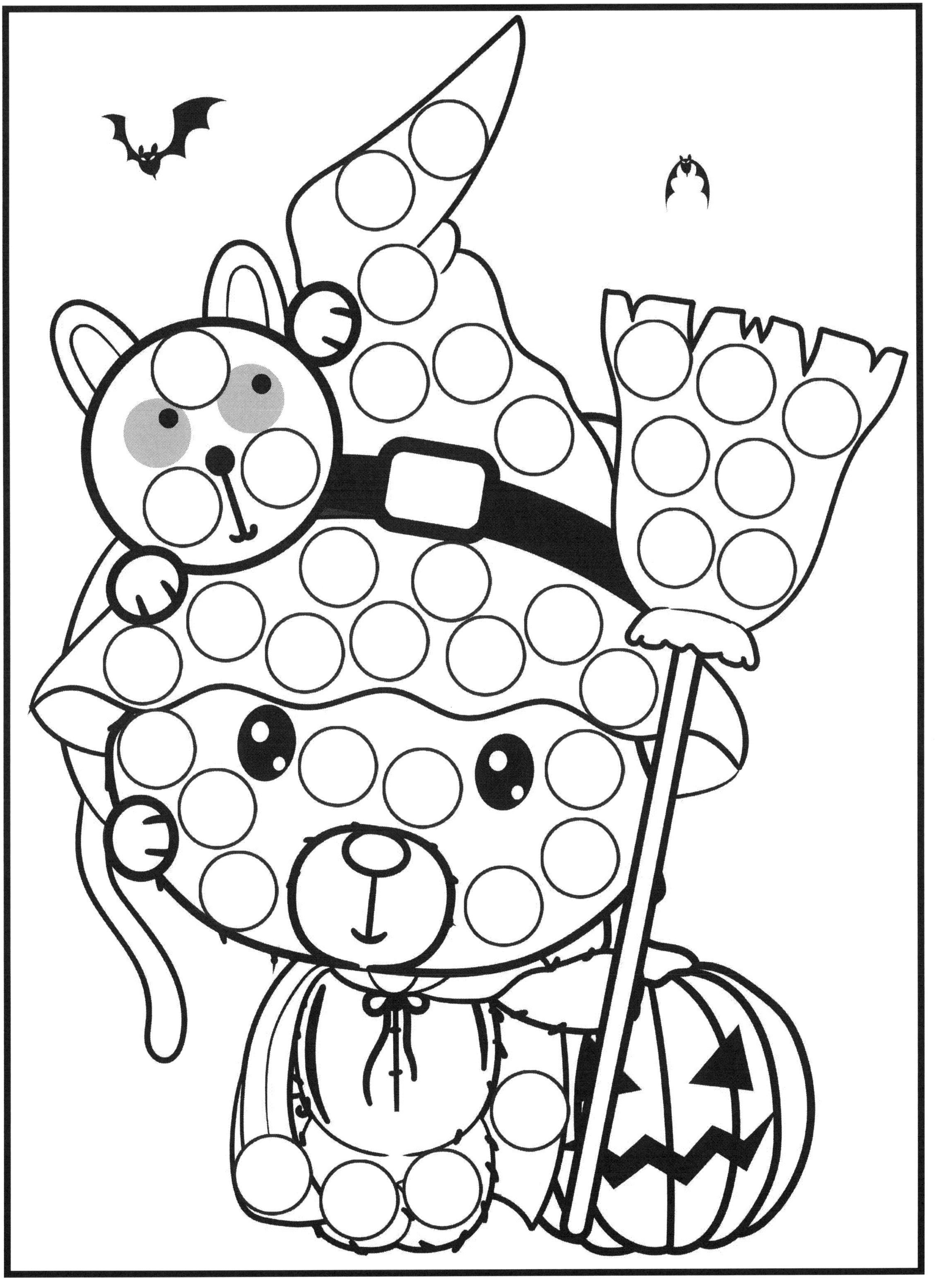

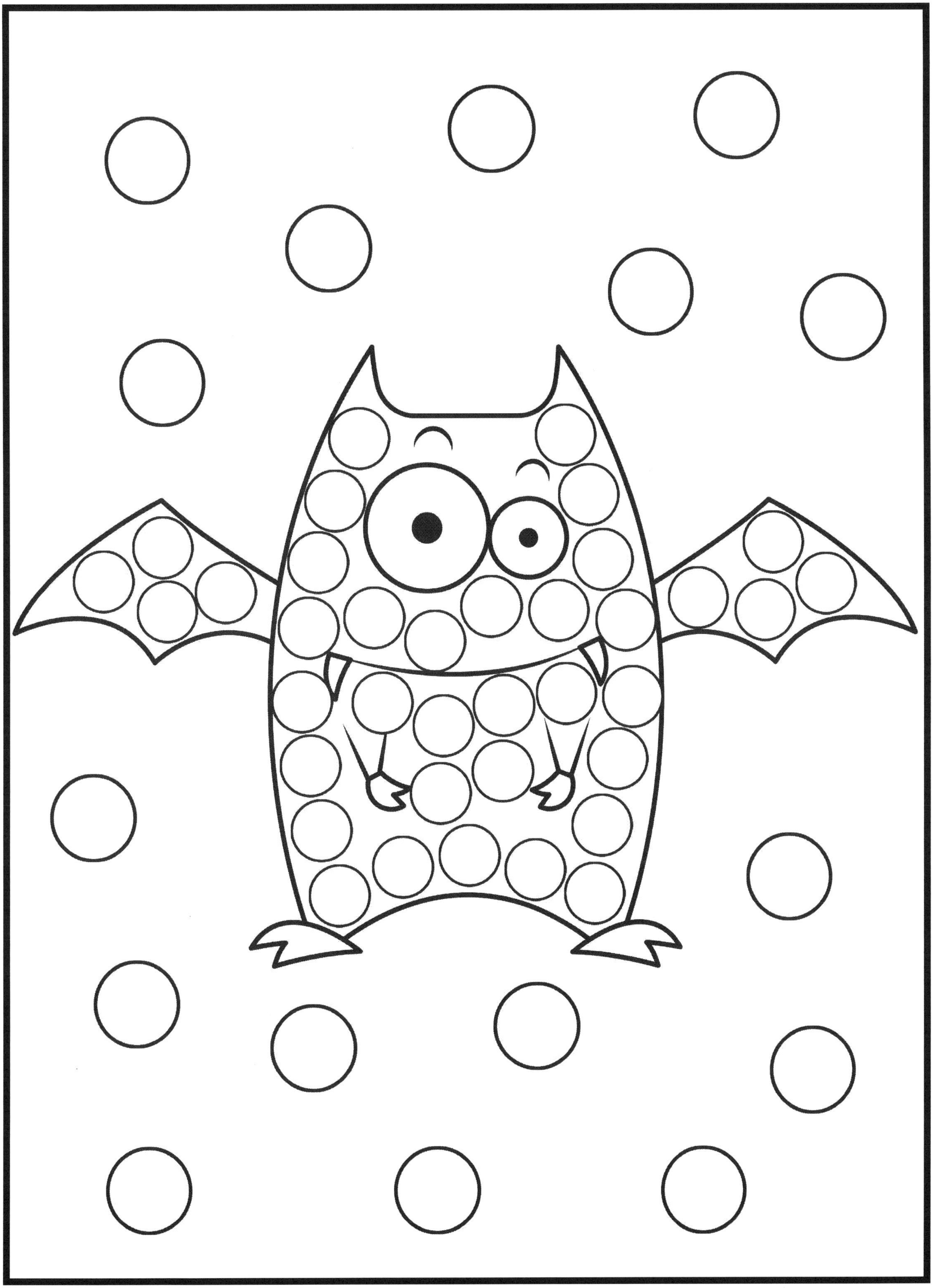

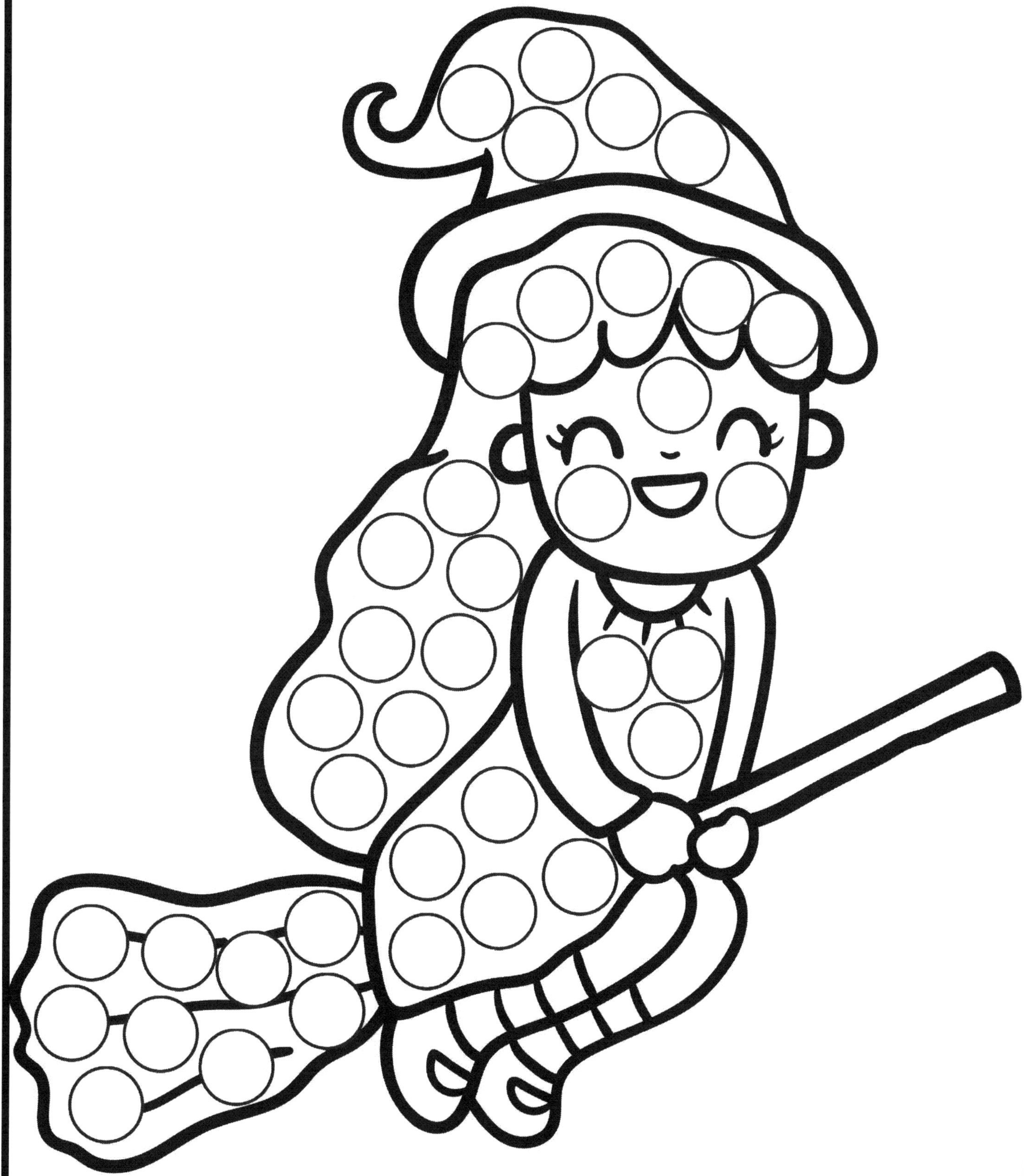

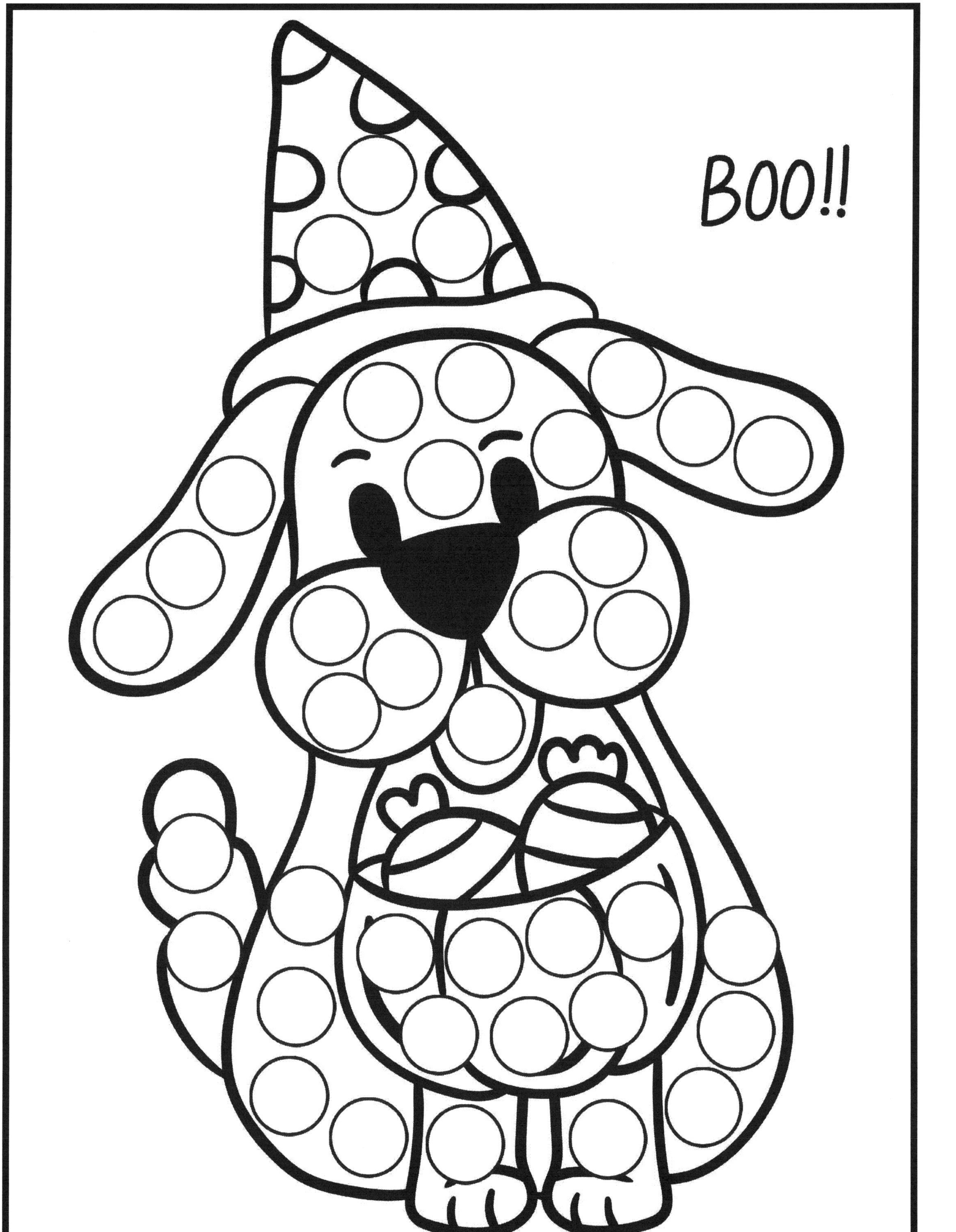
BOO!!

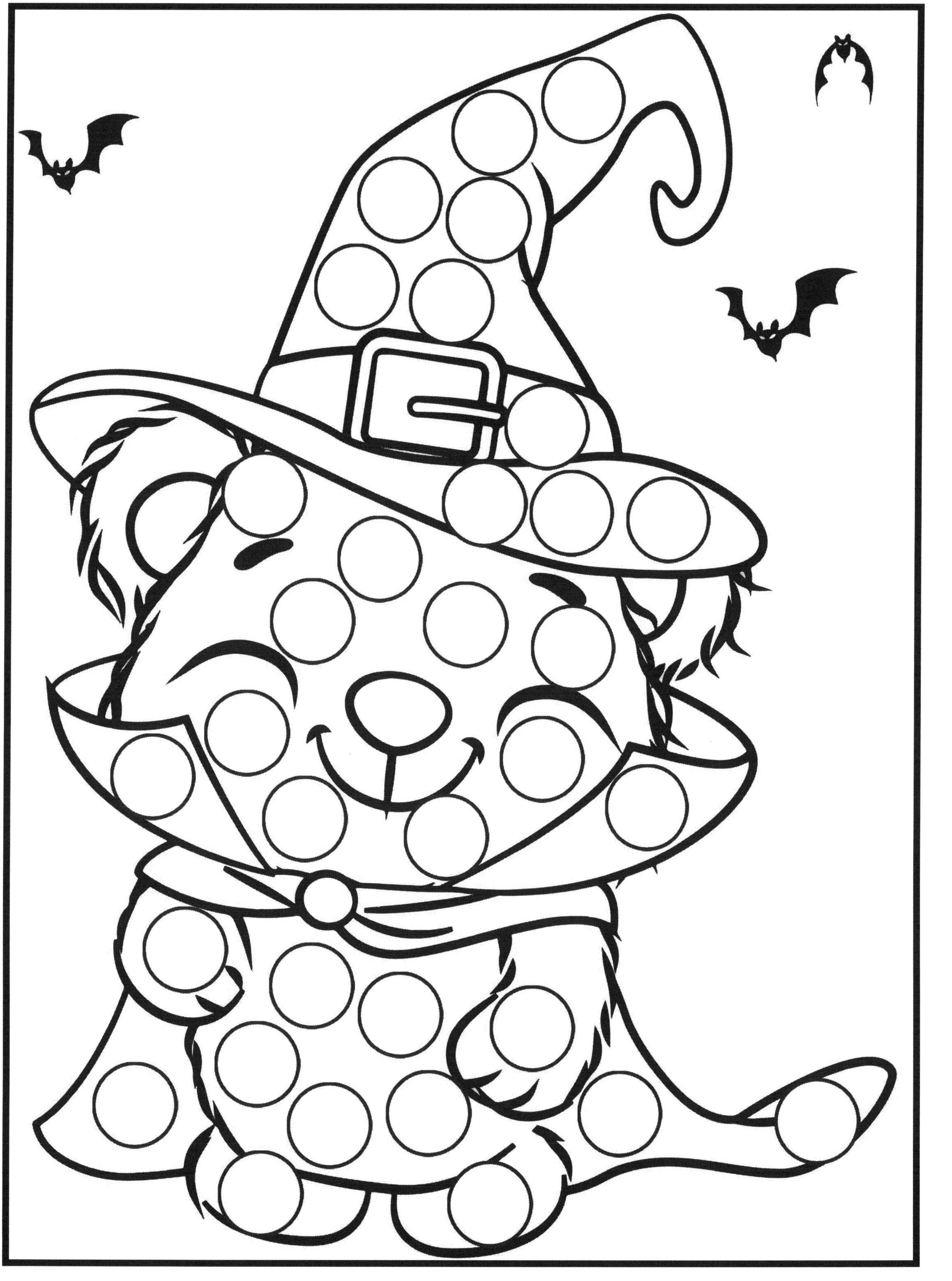

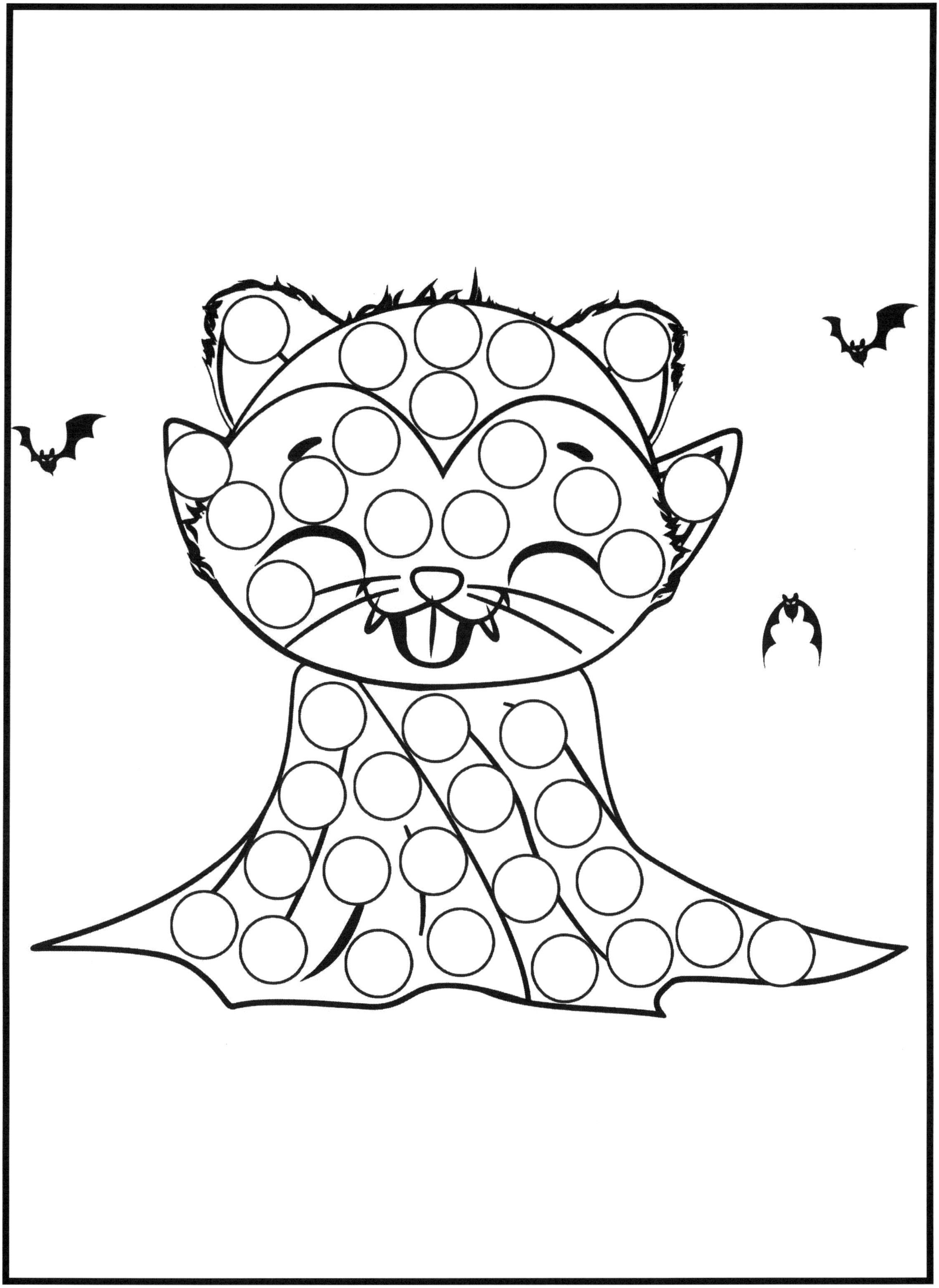

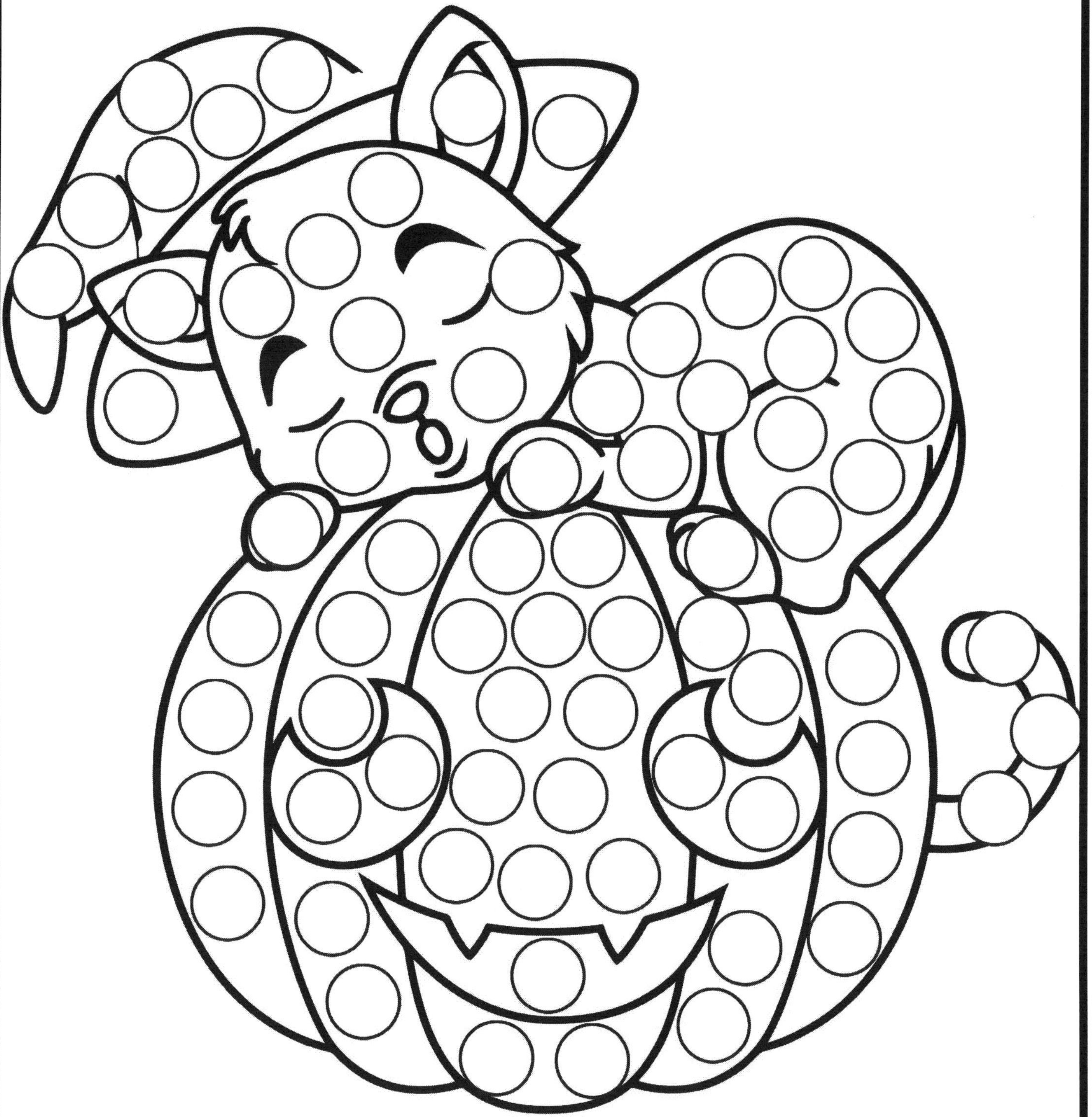

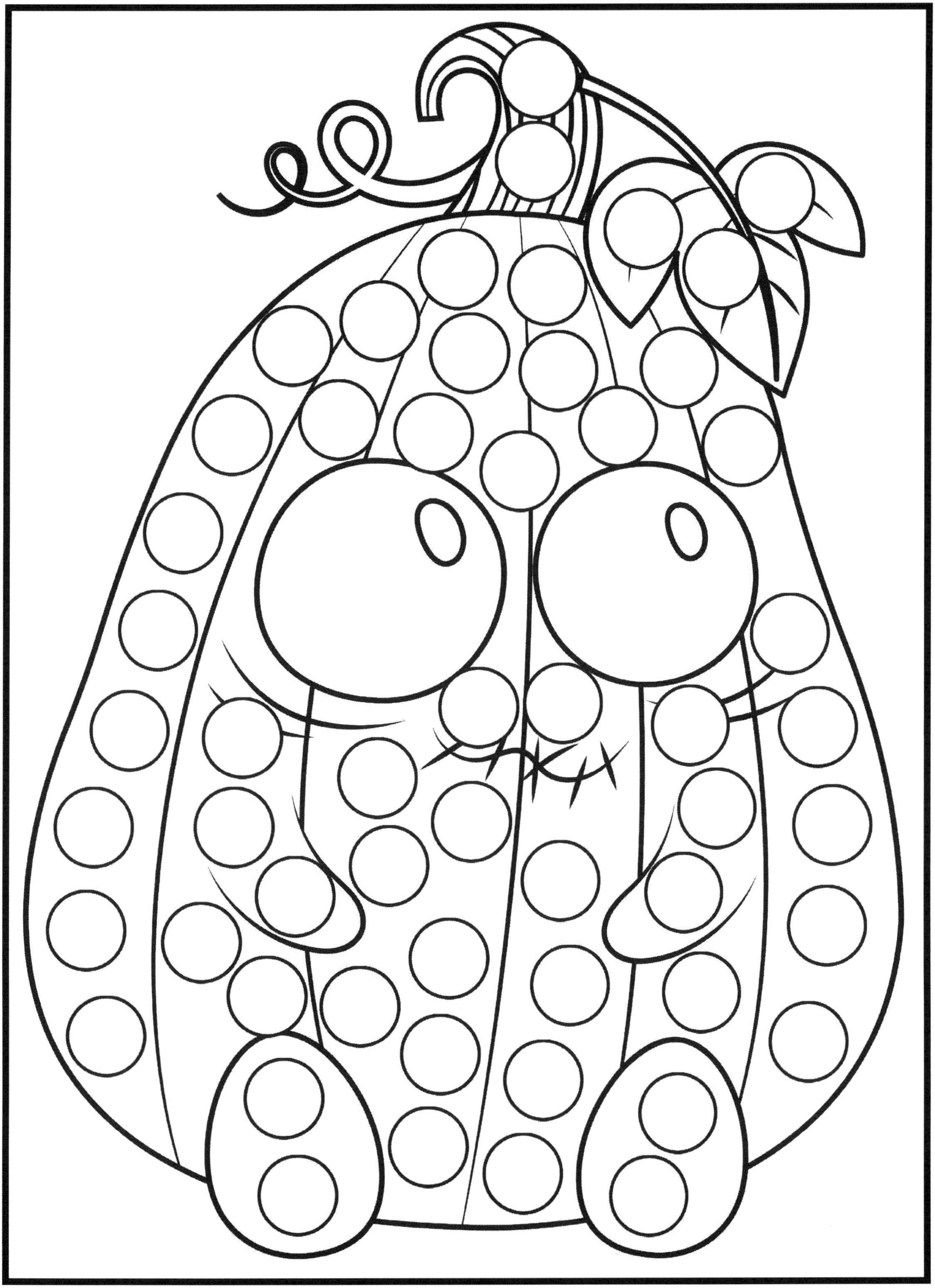

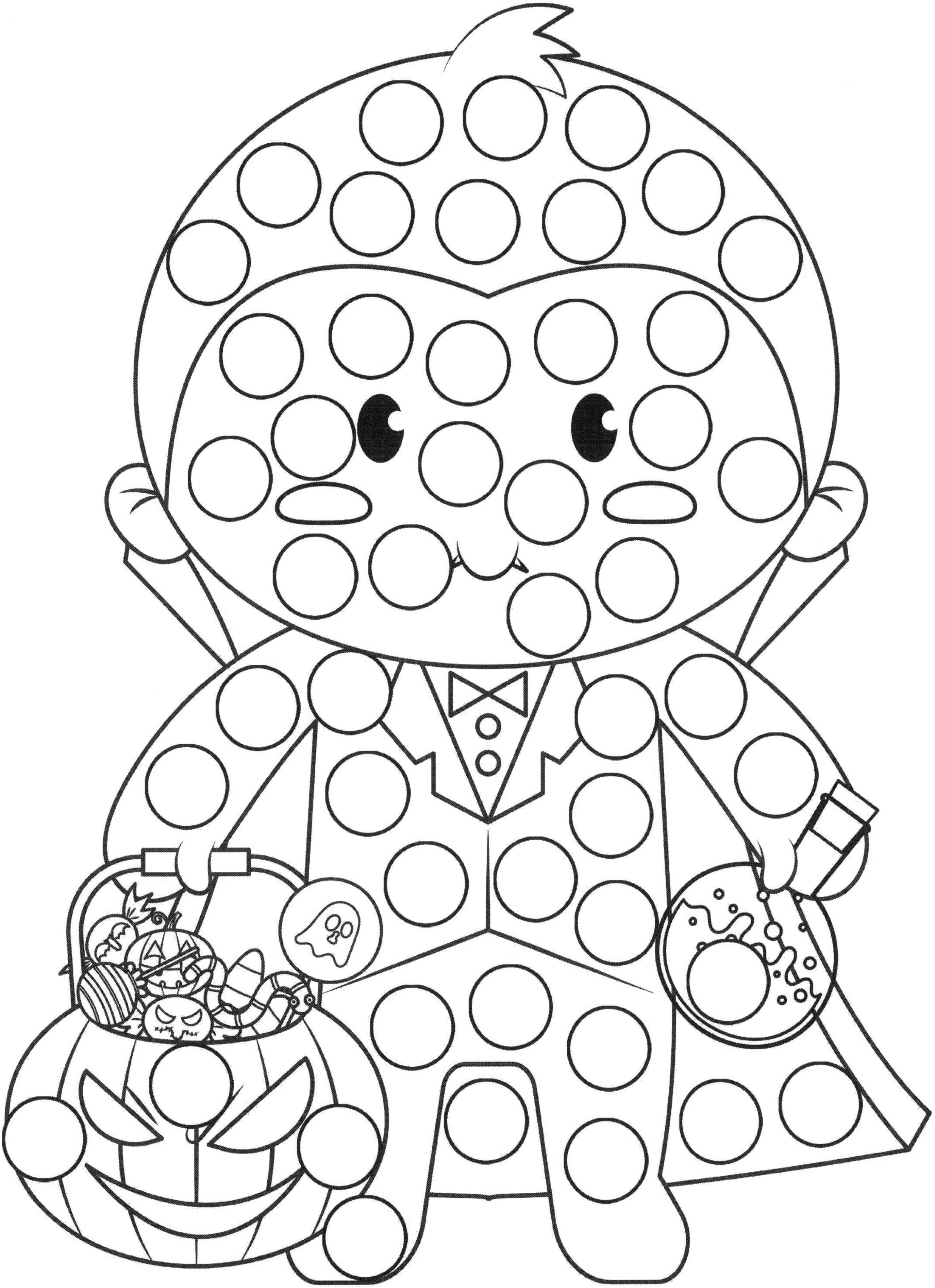

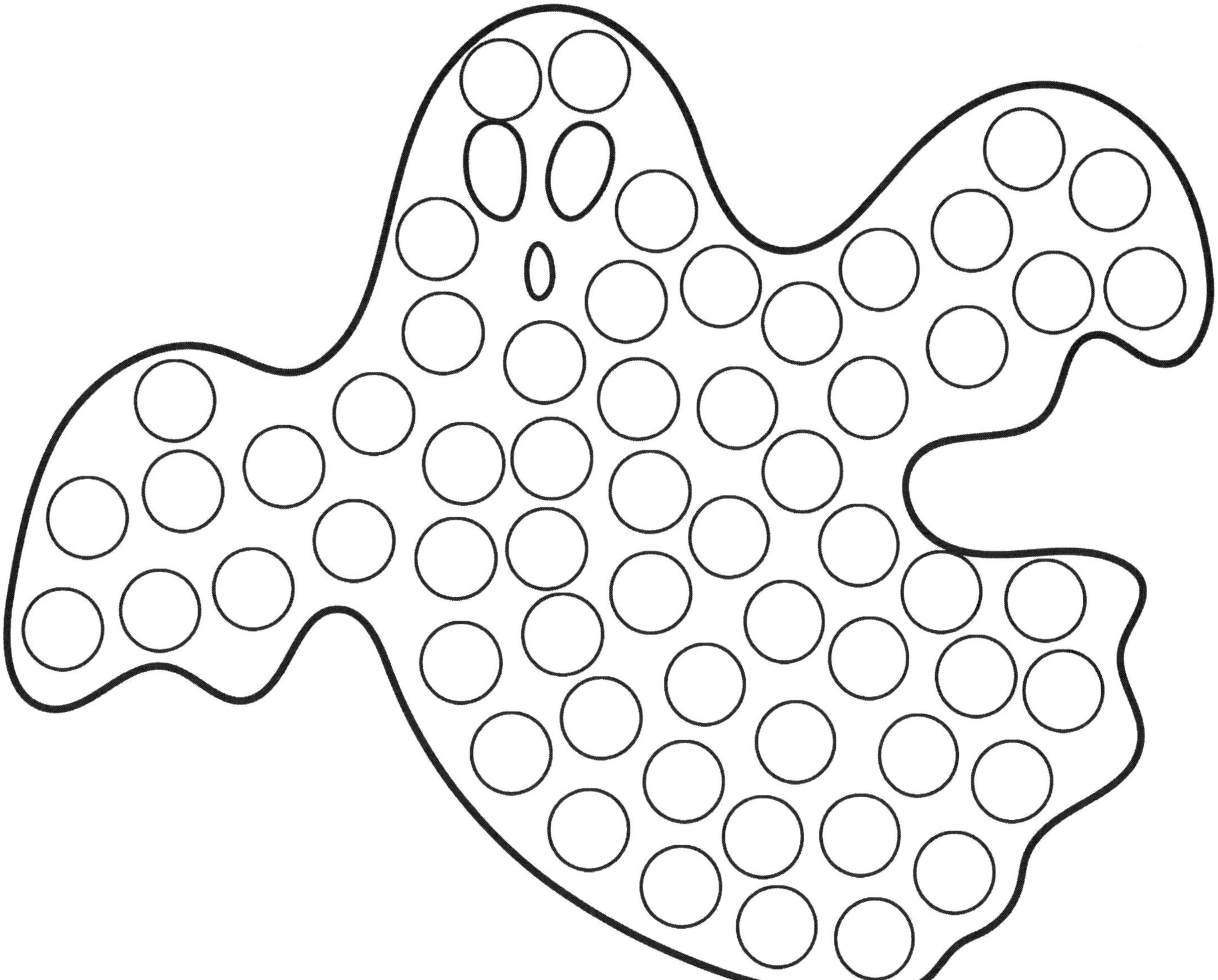

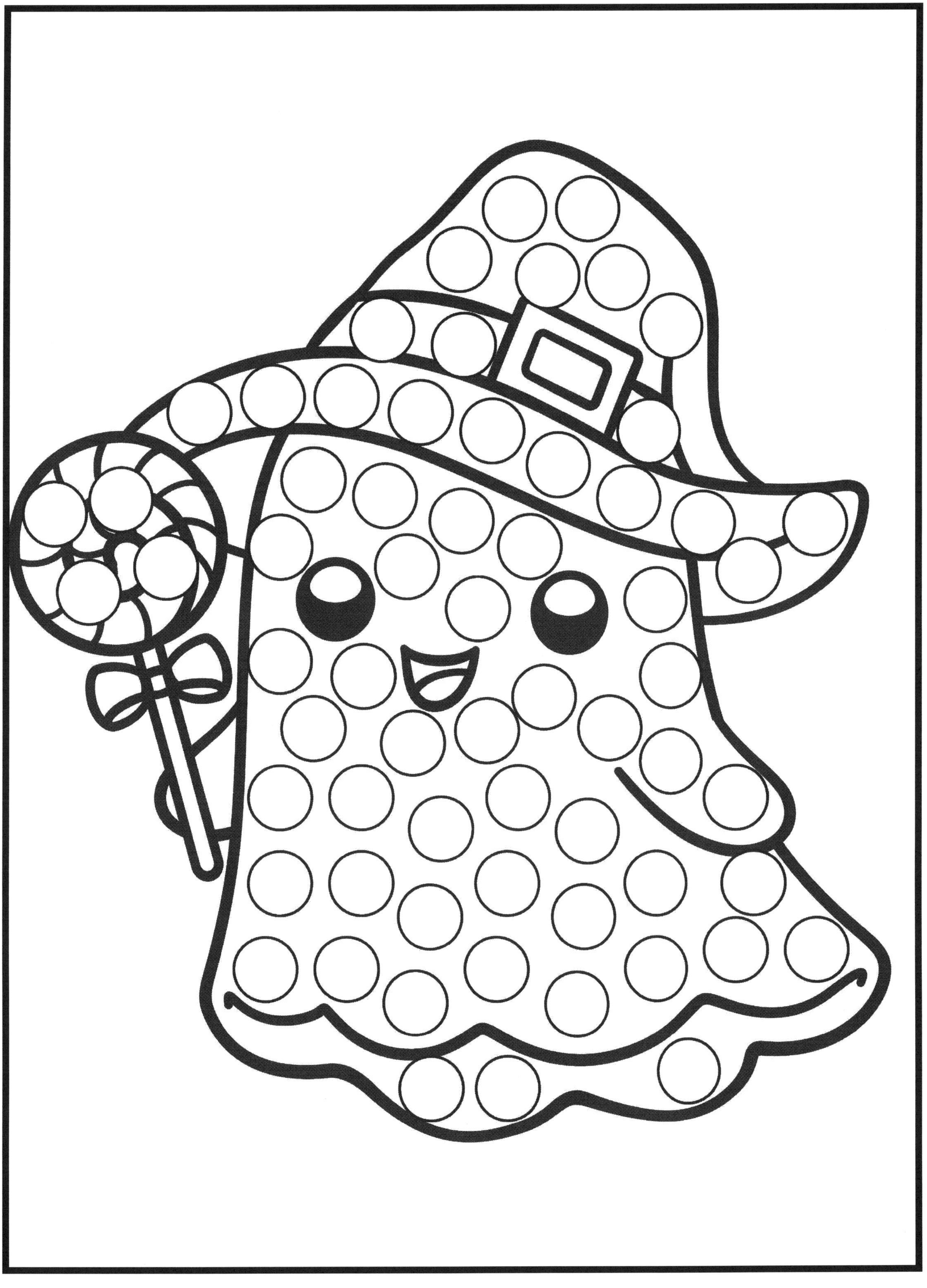

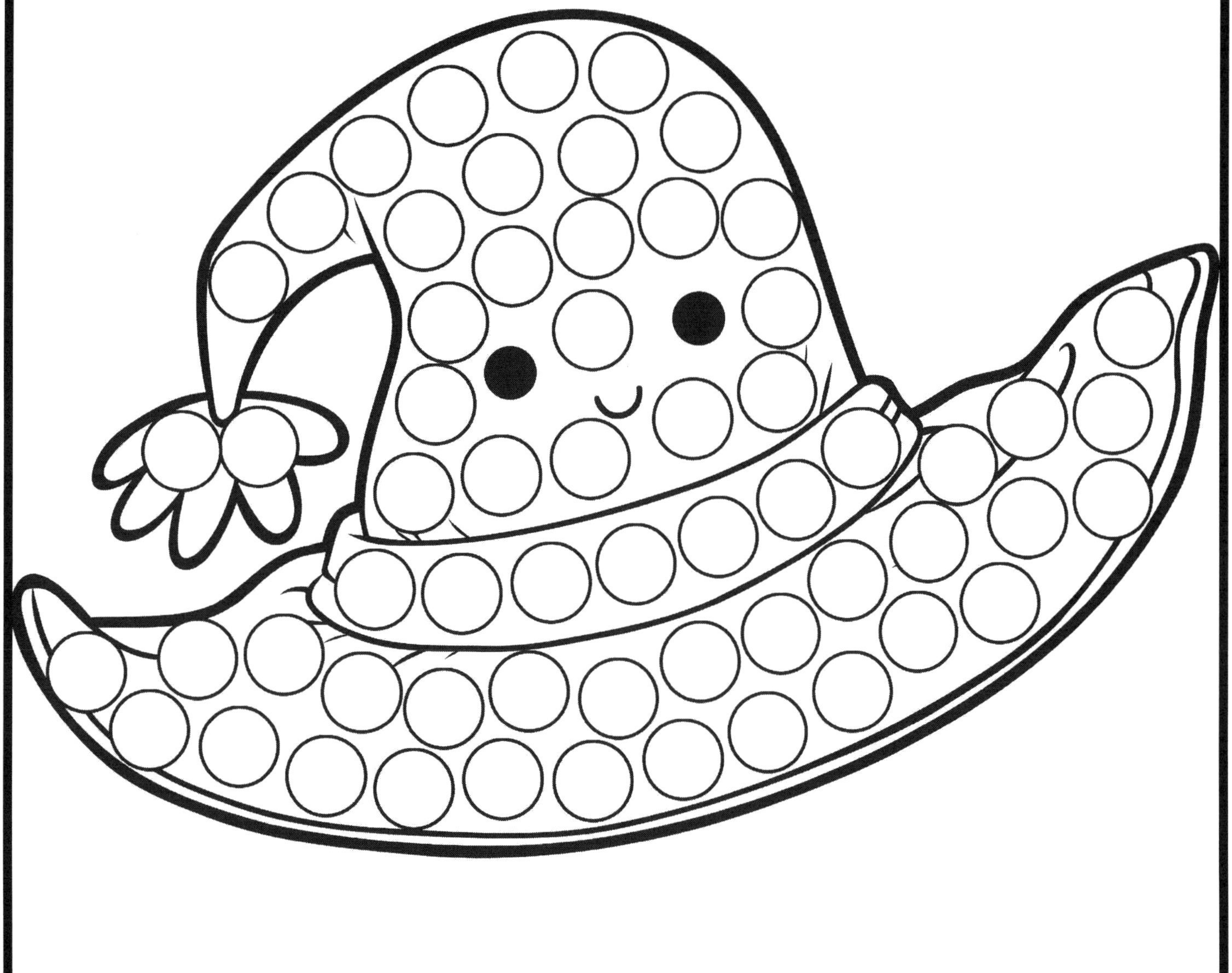

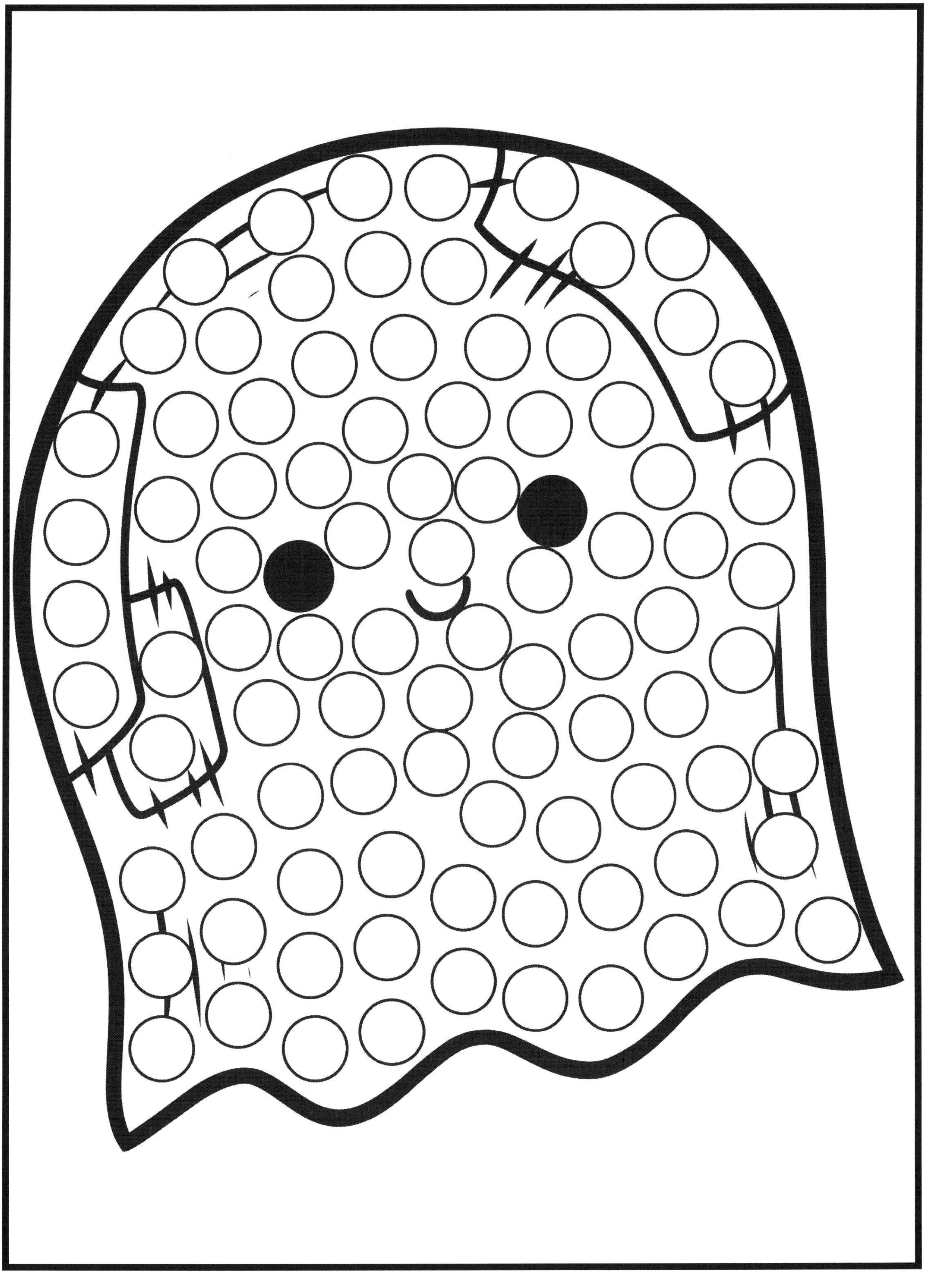

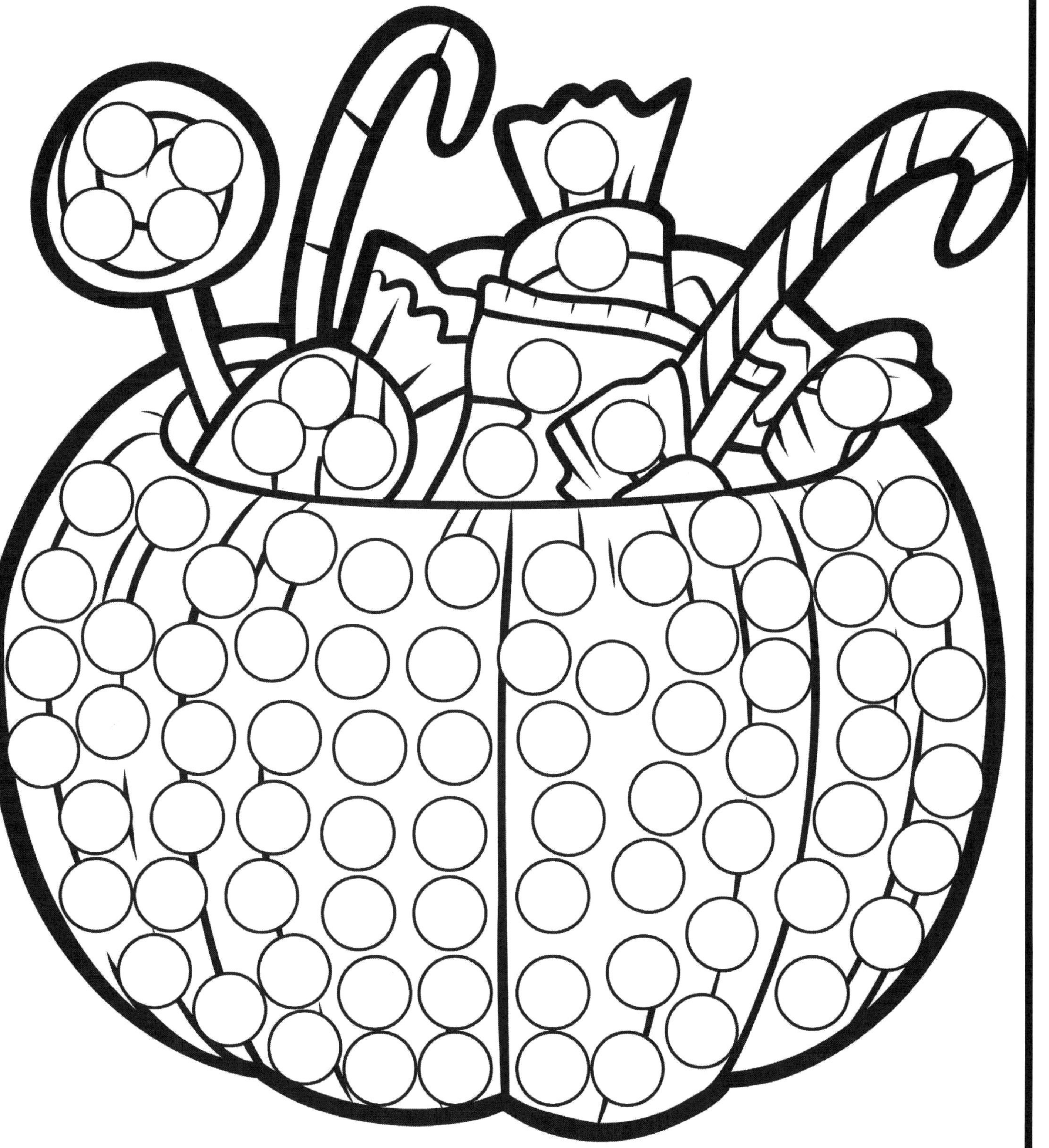

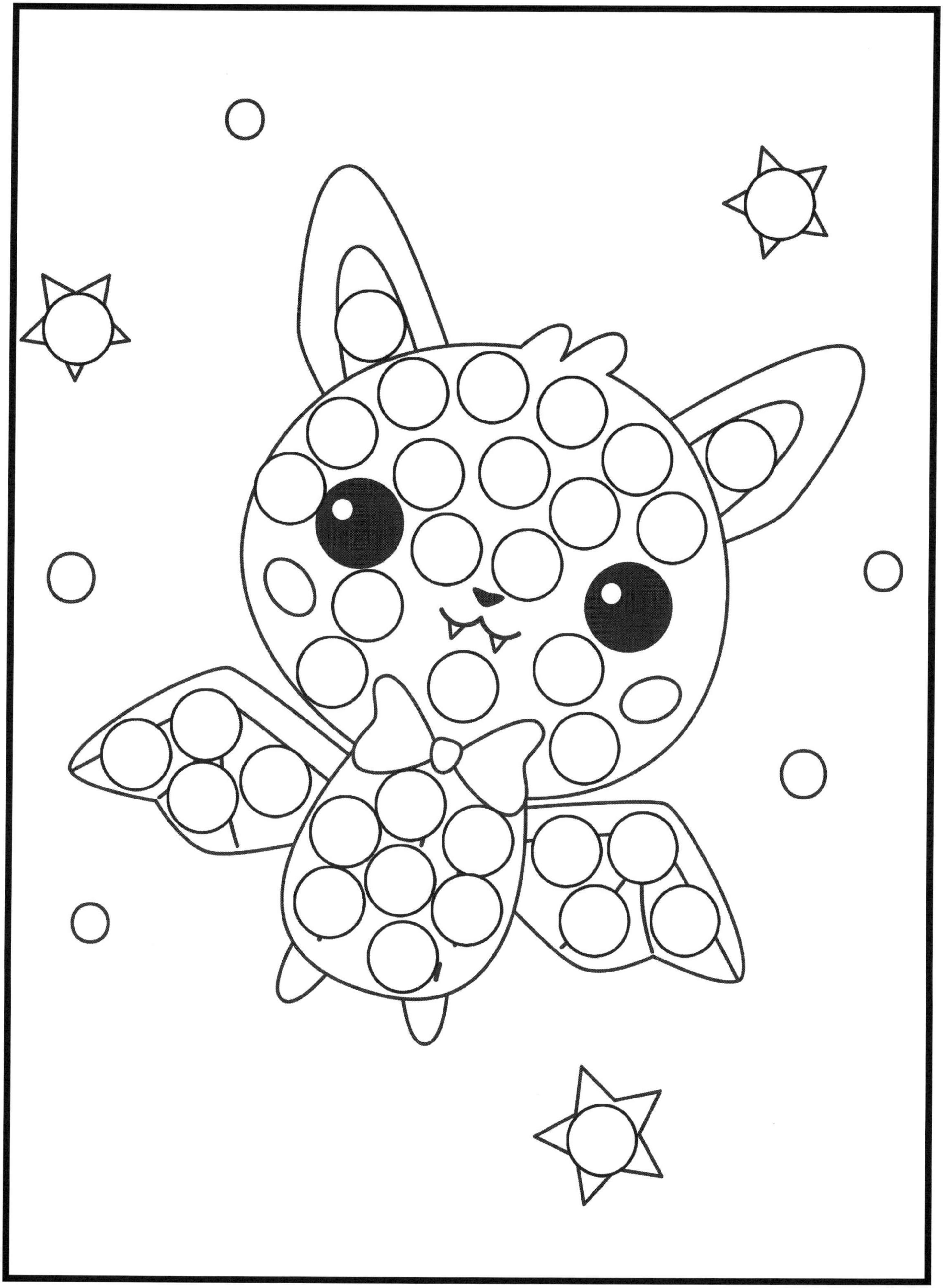

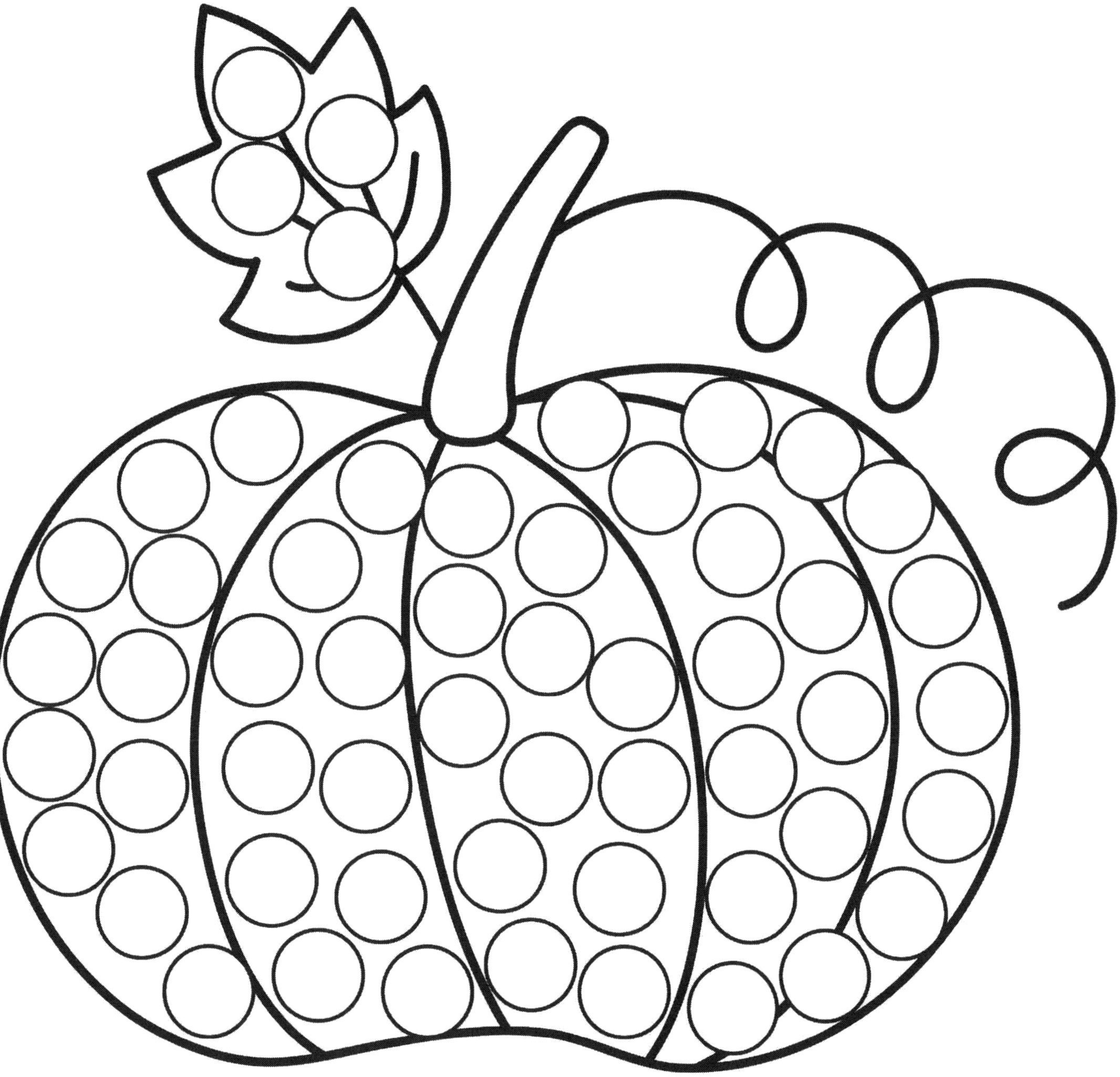

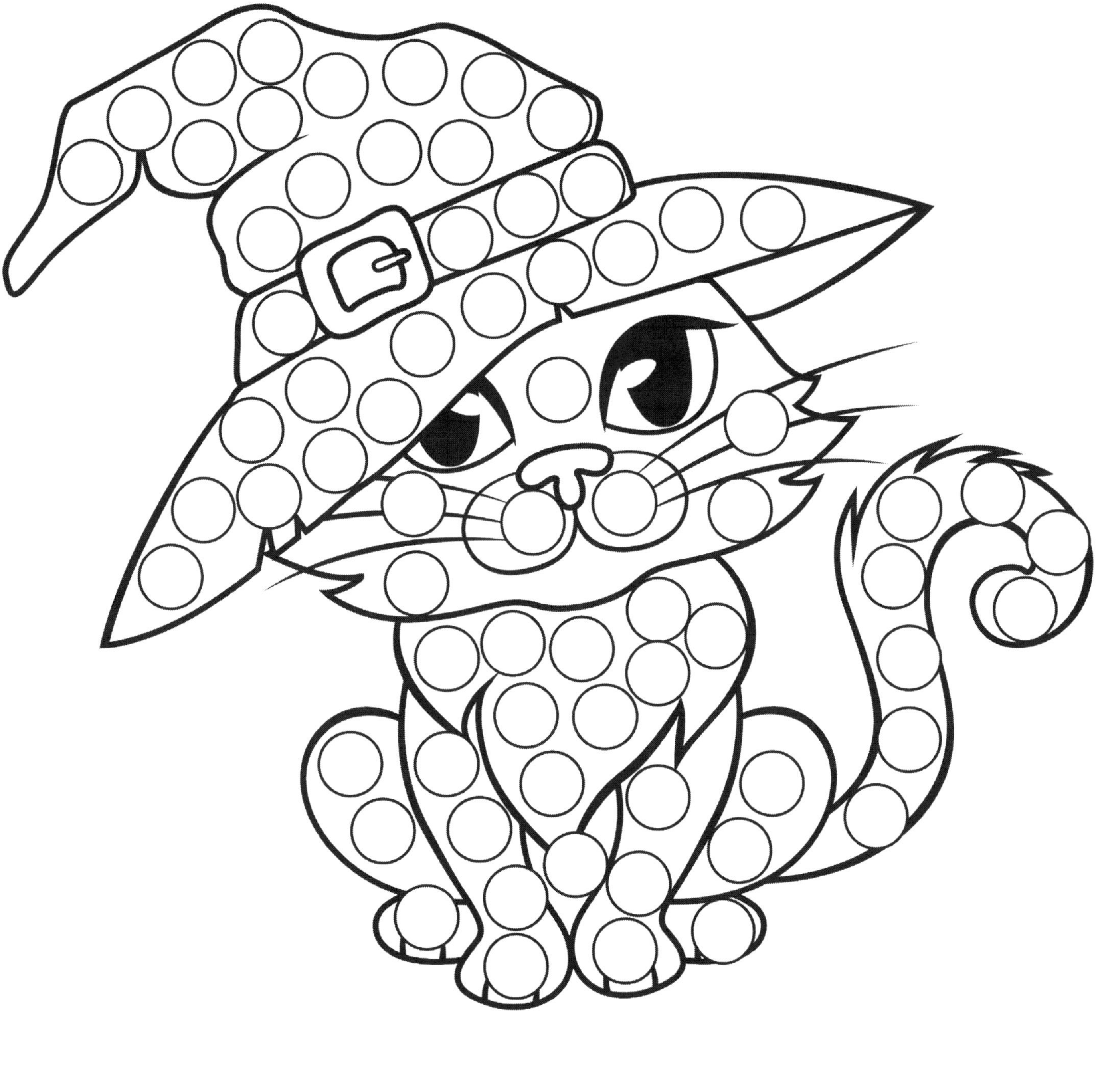

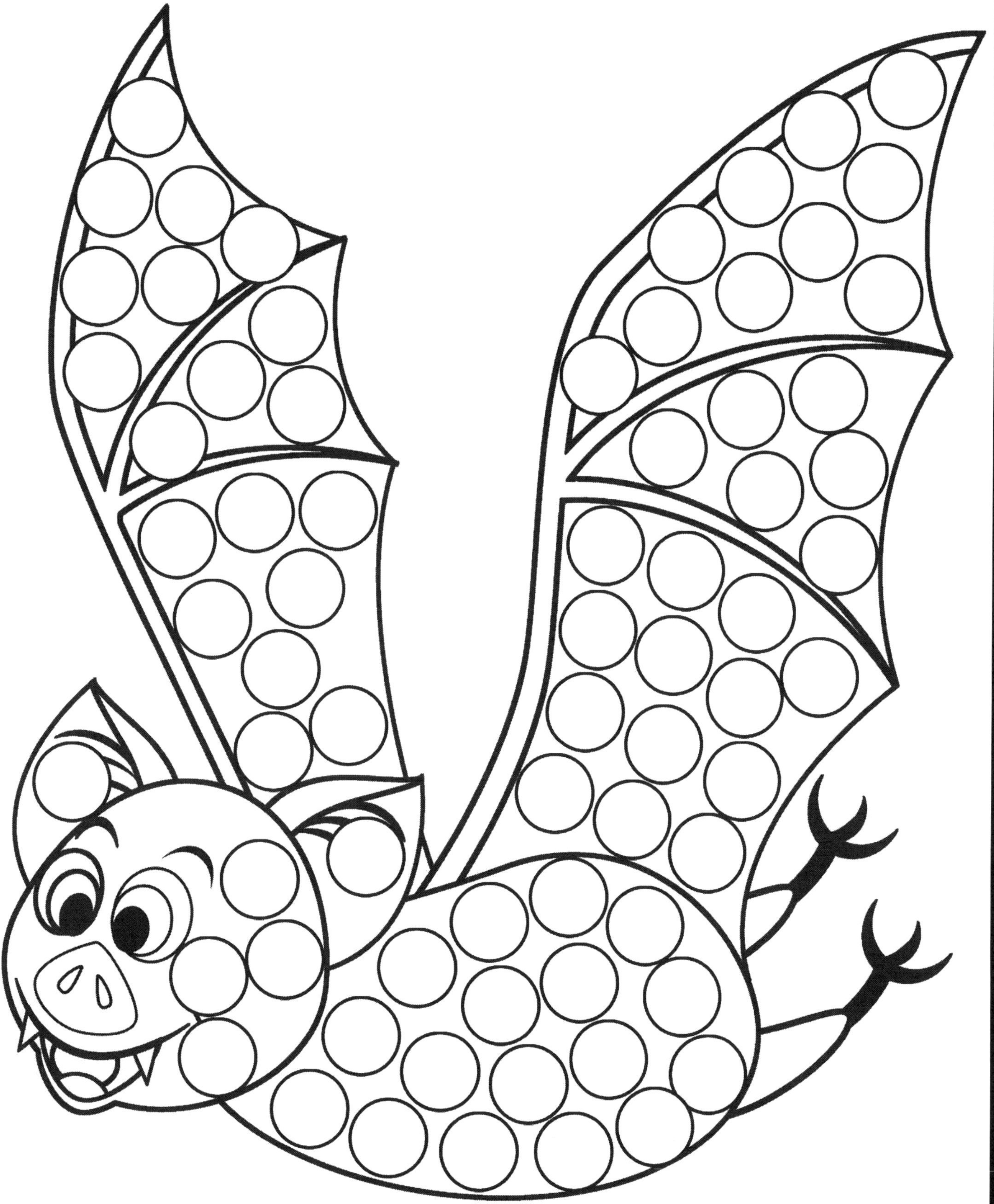

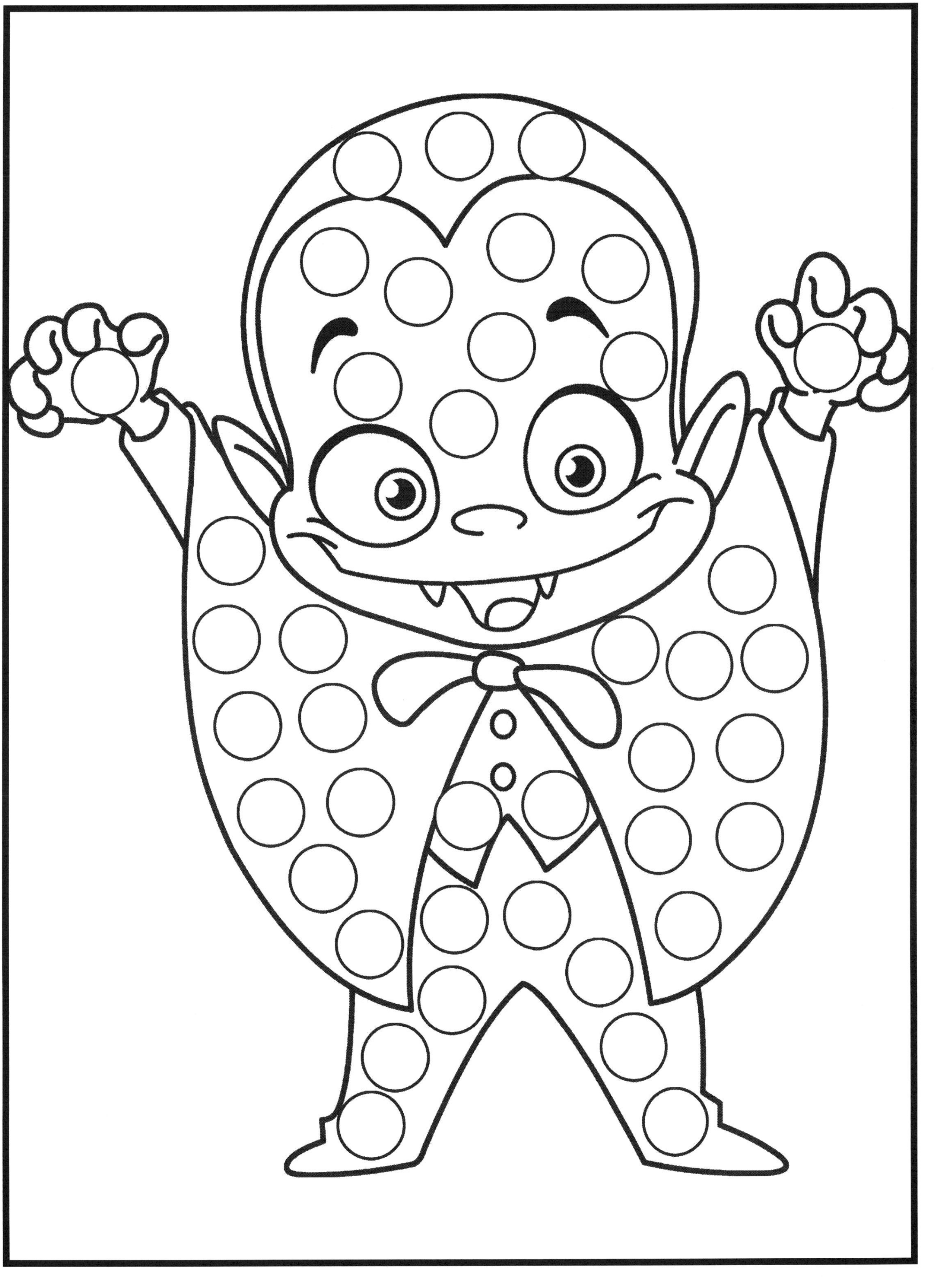

Made in the USA
Middletown, DE
24 October 2022

13392471R10035